Race, culture and counselling

Race, Culture and Counselling

Colin Lago
in collaboration with
Joyce Thompson

Open University Press
Buckingham · Philadelphia

Open University Press
Celtic Court
22 Ballmoor
Buckingham
MK18 1XW

and
1900 Frost Road, Suite 101
Bristol, PA 19007, USA

First Published 1996

A catalogue record of this book is available from the British Library

ISBN 0 335 19294 7 (pb)   0 335 19295 5 (hb)

Library of Congress Cataloging-in-Publication Data
Lago, Colin, 1944–
    Race, culture, and counselling / by Colin Lago in collaboration with
Joyce Thompson.
        p.   cm.
    Includes bibliographical references and index.
    ISBN 0–335–19294–7 (pbk.), – ISBN 0–335–19295–5
    1. Cross-cultural counseling – Great Britain.   2. Psychotherapy – Great
Britain.   I. Thompson, Joyce, 1938–   .   II. Title.
BF637.C6L33   1996   95–24920
                                                                CIP

Typeset by Type Study, Scarborough
Printed in Great Britain by Biddles Limited, Guildford and Kings Lynn

In loving memory of Barry Troyna

Contents

Dedications

The writing of this book has been made possible by the generous support of the Alec Van Berchem Trust to whom we are deeply grateful.

We wish to dedicate this book to all of the people who struggle and strive to make this world a better place for us all to live in, to all of those who have nurtured and inspired us on our personal journeys, and to those who have helped us towards writing this book.

Our gratitude also goes to our families who have supported our dreams and tolerated our absences and preoccupations caused by these concerns and the writing process.

Finally we wish to express our heartfelt thanks to Christine Davison, who has tirelessly typed and retyped the script over many versions.

List of tables and figures

Acknowledgements

The authors would like to thank the following authors, journals and publishers for permission to reproduce copyright material that is detailed below. Although every effort has been made to trace copyright holders, the authors and publishers apologize in advance for any unintentional omission or neglect and will be pleased to insert the appropriate acknowledgement in any subsequent edition of this book.

American Counselling Association for extracts from (a) Pedersen, P.B. (1987) 'Ten Frequent Assumptions of Cultural Bias in Counselling' and (b) Sue, D.W. et al. 'Multicultural Counselling Competencies and Standards: A Call to the Profession'.

John McLeod and Open University Press for passages from McLeod, J. (1993) *An Introduction to Counselling.*

Croom Helm for extracts from Tseng, W.S. in Cox, J.L. (1986) *Transcultural Psychiatry.*

Pluto Press for extracts from Fryer, P. (1984) *Staying Power: The History of Black People in Britain.*

Sage Publications for extracts from (a) Krippner, S. and Jilek, W.G. in Ward, C.A. (1989) *Altered States of Consciousness and Mental Health: A Cross Cultural Perspective* and (b) Hofstede, G. (1980) *Culture's Consequences: International Differences in Work Related Values.*

Foreword

I am extremely honoured to write the foreword to this book. I first met the authors in the fall of 1986, when we were involved in planning a bilateral conference on issues of cultural diversity and counselling in the United Kingdom and the United States. This conference spawned a professional collaboration that has established a transatlantic exchange of ideas on multicultural counselling issues and practices. The authors have become respected colleagues and valued friends.

Through our collaborative efforts we have discovered that issues of race and culture are critically important and challenging to counselling. Scores of mental health professionals in both the United Kingdom and the United States seem to be ill prepared to provide culturally appropriate counselling services to a diverse population. Many are searching for new ways to intervene successfully into the lives of people from diverse cultural backgrounds. This search is made even more urgent by demographic projections that suggest that racial and cultural diversity will have an even greater impact on both societies in the next century.

This book, therefore, is not only timely, but critical to the future of counselling theory and practice in the United Kingdom and beyond. It is an excellent synthesis of traditional and contemporary ideas related to issues of race and culture in counselling. The authors have presented in this volume a brilliant and comprehensive examination of the complex and often vexing issues that must be addressed if counselling is to be empowering, as opposed to oppressive, for individuals from minority or disenfranchised groups. While the book in its entirety is profoundly important, several chapters are worthy of special note. These chapters, in particular, raise the level of scholarship on issues of race and culture in counselling in Great Britain into an important new dimension. They include the chapters dealing with issues of race and power, cultural barriers to communication, indigenous approaches to helping, filmed cases, the culture of the counselling organization, supervision, training, and research.

No doubt, many ideas presented in these chapters and the remainder of the book will evoke strong feelings among readers. Some will become angry or defensive, while others will have their cultural ideas and experiences validated by the authors' arguments. No matter how you are personally affected, however, this book will challenge most of your assumptions about how to address appropriately the issues of counselling in a multicultural society. It will force you to move beyond your zone of professional comfort and assess your competence as a counsellor.

The work of Colin Lago and Joyce Thompson in this book makes a significant contribution to the literature on multicultural counselling. They have also helped to advance the theory base on counselling practice in the United Kingdom with their efforts. This book provides a major stimulus for the development or greater appreciation of the importance of cultural responsiveness in counsellor training and practice. It provides a new lens with which to view counselling theory and practice. The ideas presented here are an important effort in freeing counselling from the narrow confines of traditional thinking. Lago and Thompson's work provides a helping framework which allows for equal access and opportunities to all people regardless of race or culture.

Courtland Lee
Professor of Counsellor Education
University of Virginia

Introduction

This book seeks to explore some of the major dimensions and subtleties underlying the issues of race and culture and how these might impact upon counselling and psychotherapy relationships.

We have long been concerned about the nature of oppression and how discriminatory practices occur. Our professional experience within British society has exposed us directly to people, who, because of their differing cultural and or racial origins, have been discriminated against.

We have previously worked together on training projects, writing tasks and the production of a training video on this subject.

Despite the British context, many of the issues and concerns discussed here will be applicable to therapists in many other societies and cultures having culturally and racially different clients.

The climate in which the contents of this book are set, described more fully in Chapter 1, is a profoundly complex one in terms of history, population complexity, political perspectives and a huge range of cultural identities. All this is further compounded by discrimination and racism. Both counsellors and clients are participants in this climate, and as such, are subject to the multitude of complex forces and attitudes that shape people's lives.

Counsellors and psychotherapists have to acknowledge that their assumptions and beliefs about and attitudes towards those who are culturally and racially different may well be oversimplistic, judgemental and discriminatory. At worst and as a consequence, therapeutic aims may well have anti-therapeutic outcomes.

The dialogical approach of counselling and psychotherapy has now come of age alongside other healing approaches within many societies.

The challenges to counsellors are many:

- Do they understand the impact of their own past upon their assumptions about culture, identity, morals and so on?
- Do they understand the discriminatory nature and power imbalance of the

relationship between dominant and minority groups in society and how such practices are perpetuated?

- Can they enhance their own learning about the groups from which clients come?
- Are they open to a wide range of challenging and perhaps contradictory views of the world expressed by clients?
- How might their theories and models of counselling be extended or modified to incorporate a wider range of understanding and response modes to clients?
- How might their way of being with clients recognize and address the societal and political implications (as well as the emotional and psychological implications) of the client's situation?

'Counsellors are trained to work in a sensitive, skilled and theoretically informed manner with individuals seeking help.' This is the opening sentence of Chapter 2. In order to work with culturally and racially different clients, therapists will also require an understanding of how contemporary society works in relation to race, the exercise of power, the effects of discrimination, stereotyping, how ideologies sabotage policies and so on. In short, counsellors require a structural awareness of society.

A broad overview of those engaged in the counselling profession would show that many practitioners hold strongly humanitarian world views. However, counsellors are not necessarily aware of the nature or extent of the structural inequalities that so adversely affect black people's lives nor are clearly aware of their own position in those issues. For many white people who believe themselves to be tolerant, understanding, accepting and so on, it is often very difficult to appreciate the multiplicity of mechanisms in society that perpetuate systems of disadvantage amongst black people.

Chapter 3 opens with a quote stressing the complexity of the word 'culture' and continues with an examination of what differences in culture might mean. Despite very sincere attempts to understand clients' inner realities, counsellors, like all human beings, do respond initially on the basis of their own prejudices. The impact of their perception of and then judgement of difference might prevent any therapeutic progress whatsoever.

Fortunately we have experienced situations where – even though clients have had profoundly different cultural origins to ourselves – a process of counselling has been helpful. Cultural difference itself is not necessarily a barrier to effective therapy though it can cause immense confusion, because culture profoundly affects people's ways of being, their behaviour, their interpersonal relationships, their notions of meaning and so on.

When people share cultural origins and understandings, they share, often without any awareness, sufficient 'recipes' for understanding each other's present behaviour and predicting their future behaviour. Culturally different persons do not enjoy these shared assumptions, thus emphasizing the importance of therapists becoming culturally informed.

While communication constitutes part of the visible and audible aspects of people's behaviour, the inner origins of such messages come from the complex inner workings of their minds, their emotions, their memories, their relationships and so on. This book encourages counsellors to understand more fully their inner complexities and specifically their own cultural barriers to communication; the topic is specifically considered in Chapter 4.

This chapter offers a very wide range of ideas concerning cultural differences in behaviour. This considerable range of information has deliberately been included to demonstrate the enormous extent of the potential behavioural differences that could occur between counsellors and their culturally different clients.

The relationship between language, thought and experience is one of great complexity and is considered in Chapter 5. It is our view that transcultural issues must not be reduced to the limiting interpretations of the function of language and language differences.

We suggest that language has potential for infinite creativity and conveys the speaker's capacity for ingenuity, invention, and figurative, idiomatic and allusive expression. Taken from this philosophical stance, language always has the potential to express thought and to acknowledge experience. As counselling philosophy implicitly recognizes the potential for growth in people, it would seem important to understand that the nature of language within the counselling process always has the potential of achieving its task of articulating and making understandable the client's agenda.

The process of counselling, with its accent on acceptance, listening and dialogue, has the potential to provide persons from minority groups or low-esteem positions with the opportunity to speak, practice, experiment with and thus create and develop their 'word', their symbols of meaning. Counselling, in this sense, contributes to a language and a confidence derived from clients' own explorations of their situation.

This perspective demonstrates the complex relationship between language and power. If the client, through psychotherapy, develops their language or a confidence in their view of the world, much has been achieved. On the other hand, the therapist must pay attention to their own use of language and its potential negative effects upon clients. Also, counsellors must take responsibility for interacting in the language requested by the client.

Counsellors are significantly influenced in the ways they approach, reflect upon and predict the outcome of their work by the tutorial and theoretical influences they were exposed to whilst in training or in post. Many of the current theories of therapy are rooted, historically, in central European and North American cultures. Chapter 6 offers an explanation of some of these and subsequently presents some critiques where they are compared with non-western approaches.

The writings of western therapists frequently feature metaphors such as process, rhythm, dance and journey in attempting to describe their work. Positive inferences may be drawn from these perspectives in relation to therapists' interest in and capacity of openness towards other cultures, disciplines and belief systems.

The nature of persons who become psychotherapists is extremely fascinating and further complicates the relationship between theory, practice and culture as embedded in the persona of the counsellor.

The ways people cope, attempt to solve their problems and seek assistance are shaped by the social and cultural norms and the symbolic meanings within their culture. In addition, differences also exist between cultures on what is even deemed as problematic.

A matrix of healing approaches first mentioned in Chapter 1 is reintroduced in Chapter 7 and offers a conceptual model for understanding a complete range of helping interventions. This section introduces the reader to a wide range of non-Eurocentric healing methods and reminds us that long before western medicine recognized the fact, African traditional healers had taken the position that ecology and interpersonal relations affect people's health.

Healers around the world have shaped and developed 'spontaneous experiences' to arrive at highly elaborated healing systems. Meditation traditions, drum and dance-related trance-inducing systems and healing practices employing psychedelic drugs are well-known examples.

Most western therapies emphasize the individual; the healing forms described in Chapter 7 have a much more community or family focus.

We have to recognize this breadth and complexity of spectrum of healing approaches embedded in all societies and note that each has its validity within the cultural frameworks from which it originates. In addition, there are often similarities between the forms of activity used by different cultures, e.g. trance states, though the rituals may be differently structured.

Chapter 8 offers a series of transcripts taken from transcultural counselling interviews that may be used for training and discussion purposes.

Historically the literature on transcultural counselling has substantially ignored organizational and systemic issues. Chapter 9 attempts to confront this vacuum by considering the nature of the organizational context within which counselling takes place. The location within which the therapy takes place might be, for some clients, as important as the therapy itself.

All cultures have conventions influenced both by codes and practices related to hospitality. These conventions influence both design and layout of buildings as well as informing interpersonal behaviours. The whole of Chapter 9 is concerned with stimulating a consideration of how counselling organizations can create the conditions (physical, psychological and emotional) within which successful therapy can occur.

Supervision, training and research are the subjects of the final three chapters. Each of these facets that prepare, support and underpin therapist practice have immense significance for the development of transculturally sensitive and skilled therapists. These elements overlay a deep concern for ethical and effective therapeutic practice in the interests of all clients living in multicultural and multiracial societies.

We are concerned that counselling and psychotherapy does not become a further oppressive or damaging instrument of society, but that it continues to aspire to be an appropriately liberating and therapeutic force for any troubled individuals, families or groups seeking psychological help and emotional support.

We have deliberately used various terms interchangeably within this book in relation to the helping or therapeutic process. We are aware of the current debate about differences between counselling and psychotherapy. Our concern here, whatever these differences are, is to address all who aspire, through the skills of listening, relating and dialogue, to relieve others' suffering. We hope that the various terms used, for example, counsellor, counselling, psychotherapist, therapist, psychotherapy and so on, facilitate easy reading.

There are also a range of terms used in the book to describe the activity of counselling a client from another racial or cultural background. In recent times these terms have included 'crosscultural', 'intercultural', 'transcultural' and 'multicultural'. In most instances we have used the conventions of 'transcultural', a term increasingly popular in British literature and 'multicultural', a term current within the United States.

Similarly we have used terms such as 'culturally different', 'racially different', 'black and white' as variously descriptive of counsellors and clients. Where we have used the terms 'black and white' we intend these to be interpreted in their political sense, where blackness is used to describe those who are not the traditional power holders or members of a dominant majority group in a society.

Language can age very quickly and connotative meanings may thus swing from having positive to negative effects. Consequently we have avoided giving precise definitions and interpretations to these terms. We encourage, rather, the reader to appreciate our attempts to address the lived complexity of such helping relationships, whatever the current definitions are.

1

The climate, the context and the challenge

The climate: the multicultural and multiracial nature of society today

The multicultural and multiracial composition of British society today is enormously complex. Inevitably, any systematic analysis of a population will rest upon the nature of how people and groups are categorized and to what extent they enjoy temporary or permanent residence.

Let us consider some of these complexities. Whilst living in Leicester during the 1980s one of the authors came across a survey of city residents that revealed 43 different countries of origin in that one city alone. At Sheffield University, where that author now works, there were 2,300 international students in 1994 coming from 104 countries. Indeed in terms of international students, it has been estimated that, currently, between 80,000 and 100,000 temporarily reside in Britain to pursue higher education (Morgan and Bo 1993).

Categorization of different groups in society is a problem-strewn activity. Skellington and Morris (1992) include a complete chapter in their book on the 'construction of racial data'. They point out that racial categories or racial groups do not exist as objective biological facts in any meaningful way. The study of human beings has been unable to identify significant characteristics that can be found in some groups of people but not in others that would allow us to delineate distinct racial groups. Such studies have not found any differences of ability or intelligence.

Nationalities of origin might be a more reliable measure to use, in that these reflect a legal status: however such measures do not account for groups that are legally and residentially British. Even the national census changed the way it categorized people between the 1971 and 1991 surveys.

In April 1991 there were nearly four million people resident in the UK who were born elsewhere, 7.3 per cent of the population (Sanders 1994).

The term 'immigrant' has for many become synonymous with being black. However, the majority of immigrants are white, from Eire, the old

Table 1.1 Overseas-born population of Great Britain 1971

Country of birth	Resident in Great Britain
Total Ireland	709,235
Irish Republic	615,820
Ireland (part not stated)	93,415
Total New Commonwealth countries	1,151,090[1]
Nigeria	28,565
Barbados	27,055
Guyana	21,070
Jamaica	171,775
Trinidad and Tobago	17,135
Cyprus	73,292
Hong Kong	29,520
India	321,995
Pakistan	139,935
Malta and Gozo	33,840
Total European countries	632,770
Germany	157,680
Italy	108,980
Poland	110,925
Spain	49,470
Total other countries	979,990
America	131,540
China	13,495
USSR	48,095
Turkey	6,615

Notes:
[1] This figure includes people from Australia, New Zealand and Canada.
[2] The table provides various regional totals and then details some of the largest sources of overseas-born population, by country, within these regions. The total figures are therefore not a summation of the figures listed below them.
Source: Census 1971, Great Britain, Country of Birth Tables quoted in Rees 1982, p. 76.

Commonwealth (Australia, New Zealand and Canada) and from other European countries. The 1981 census revealed that 3.4 million people in Britain were born overseas: of those 1.9 million were white. Owen's analysis of the 1991 census reveals that 61 per cent of immigrants are white (Owen 1993). The same source reveals that the southern Irish still form the largest category of non-native residents though their numbers had dropped by 12 per cent between 1981 and 1991. During this period the number of British residents born in Bangladesh had increased by 116 per cent, those born in Japan by 130 per cent and Turkey by 125 per cent. The survey also noted that just over 28,000 Japanese people were now resident in this country.

Table 1.1 shows the overseas-born population of Great Britain taken from the 1971 survey.

Skellington and Morris (1992), using figures taken from the labour force survey reports published by the Office of Population Censuses and Surveys, indicate that almost one person in 20 living in Great Britain belongs to a minority ethnic group. For the period 1986–8, these surveys estimated the minority ethnic group population to be 2.58 million or 4.7 per cent of the total British population (p. 36). Projections towards the end of the century indicate that the proportion of black people in the total population of Britain will stabilize at around 6 per cent (p. 48).

In terms of both culture and race, the above snapshot of contemporary Britain serves to reveal a population that has a myriad of origins and a huge range of subcultures. As we shall see later, these groups experience different life opportunities and realities within Great Britain.

A brief historical perspective

West Africans probably first appeared in London in 1554 (Jordan 1982). This was before potatoes, tobacco or tea were brought to Britain and ten years before Shakespeare was born (Fryer 1994). Their presence reflected the developing trading opportunities at that time between Britain and West Africa. Some West Africans were brought to London to develop their language skills in order to assist the trading process and some were sold as household servants. The predominant purpose of these contacts was that of trading, as extensive English participation in the slave trade did not develop until well into the seventeenth century.

By the middle of the eighteenth century, however, Britain had become the leading slave-trading nation in the world and the centre of what was known as the triangular trade. Her ships carried manufactured goods to West Africa, transported slaves to the New World and brought back sugar, tobacco and cotton to Britain. In July 1757, 175 ships with cargo worth £2 million docked in British ports. In terms of population, by 1770, in London alone, there were 18,000 black slaves, forming nearly 3 per cent of an estimated population of 650,000 (Hiro 1971).

Jordan (1982) and Hiro (1971) describe from historical accounts several dimensions that reflect white people's perceptions of black people that continue to be perpetuated today, several hundred years later. These include skin colour, religion, savage behaviour, libidinous men, black people as workhorses and so on. The attitudes that fuel contemporary prejudice often have a very long history.

The last two centuries have also seen considerable immigration from Ireland and other European countries. During the nineteenth century the largest group of immigrants to settle in England were the Irish. By 1841 there were more than 400,000 living in England, Scotland and Wales; the 1851 census showed that there were 727,326 Irish immigrants in Britain (Rees 1982: 75).

Britain experienced considerable Jewish immigration in the decades preceding the First World War. An estimated Jewish population of some 60,000 in 1880 had increased to approximately 300,000 by 1920 (Rees 1982).

Just after the Second World War a sizeable number of Polish immigrants (120,000) were accepted into Britain under the Polish Resettlement Act of 1947. Rees notes that this Act was one of the few constructive legislative initiatives in the field of immigration, a field that has been dominated by ways to keep people out (specifically black people) rather than allowing them in. Other frequently represented national groups immigrating at this time were Lithuanians, Ukrainians, Latvians and Yugoslavs (approximately 100,000) though their treatment by the authorities was substantially different and indeed worse than the Poles (p. 82).

The largest groups of postwar economic immigrants (1948 onwards) came from the poorer Commonwealth territories of the Caribbean, the Indian subcontinent, the Mediterranean and the Far East. Under the British Nationality Act of 1948 citizens of the British Commonwealth were allowed to enter Britain freely, to find work, to settle and to bring their families. Indeed, many chose to take this option as a result of employer and government-led recruitment schemes.

However, successive immigration policies since the 1960s have significantly reduced the immigration possibilities of persons specifically from the New Commonwealth and Pakistan (i.e. predominantly black people).

> Immigrants represent a declining proportion of Britain's minority ethnic group population. Nine out of every ten minority ethnic group children aged under 5 were born in the U.K. In 1984, the third P.S.I. survey estimated that 40 per cent of Britain's black population was British born; moreover P.S.I. further estimated that 50 per cent of those who came to Britain as immigrants had lived in Britain for over 15 years.
>
> (Brown 1984: 2)

Disadvantage, discrimination and racism

Towards the end of 1993 a public survey was conducted on racial harmony in Britain. One in every four white Britons, it found, would not wish to have a non-white person living next door to them. Arabs, Pakistanis, Africans, West Indians and Jews were cited as groups of people Britons would not wish to have as their neighbours (Jumaa 1993).

In 1984 the first British social attitudes survey described a British society that was seen by more than 90 per cent of the adult population to be racially prejudiced against its black and Asian members (Jowell et al. 1984). More than one third classified themselves as racially prejudiced: 42 per cent also thought racial prejudice would be worse in five years' time.

In 1992 the Runnymede Trust and the National Opinion Poll produced the findings of the largest national study of attitudes to racism since the mid-1980s and found that two out of every three white people thought Britain was a very or fairly racist society compared to four out of five Afro-Caribbeans and 56 per cent of Asians.

Moving from these recent sets of findings to a slightly more historical perspective, much evidence can be found of aggressive behaviour towards non-white groups in the United Kingdom. In 1919, for example, there was a series of attacks on black people in the docks areas of Britain: Cardiff, Glasgow, Liverpool, Hull, Manchester and London. In the 1940s there were attacks in Liverpool (1948), Deptford (1949) and Birmingham (1949). In the late 1950s black people became a particular target for racist white youths. The 1960s brought 'paki-bashing' and attacks by white 'skinheads'. The 1970s saw racial violence and harassment escalate. Evidence suggests that the situation worsened in the 1980s (Skellington and Morris 1992) and indeed the number of reported attacks rose to 8,779 in 1993, an increase of nearly 1,000 over the previous year. Unreported incidents are estimated to be as high as 150,000 (*Guardian* 18 March 1994). The Home Affairs Committee in its 1986 report, *Racial Attacks and Harassment*, accepted as its starting point that: 'the most shameful and dispiriting aspects of race relations in Britain is the incidence of racial attacks and harassment' (Home Affairs Committee 1986: 22).

Sadly, the adjectives 'shameful' and 'dispiriting' apply to all aspects of socio-cultural life. Accounts and reports of disadvantage, discrimination and racism are repeated with nauseating frequency. The issues are rife in housing, immigration, health, education, the media, criminal justice, social services and the labour market – as the following data demonstrate.

Immigration

In the early seventeenth century Queen Elizabeth I issued a decree 'to rid this land of all blackamoores'. That continuing sentiment has been a strong influence in much of the resulting immigration policy in the last hundred years. Indeed, Skellington and Morris (1992: 50) assert that 'understanding immigration policy is central to understanding racism in British society'. Many governments have passed a variety of Acts and laws that have 'provided a legal framework for the institutionalisation of racism' (Allen 1973). Many of these laws have underpinned the equation between blackness and notions of being 'second class' and 'undesirable'. This has led on to the notion that 'black people are in themselves a problem and the fewer we have of them the better'. (Ben-Tovim and Gabriel 1982). Just one example of immigration law practice, as determined in part by the various laws and the attitudes exacerbated by them, is given below.

In 1990 the refusal rate for Guyanese visitors to Britain was 1 in 87 compared, for example, with 1 in 3,600 for Norwegians (Skellington and Morris 1992). A similar startling differential was discovered in 1982 when findings by the Joint Council for the Welfare of Immigrants and the National Council for Civil Liberties compared visitors from Ghana and Sweden: Ghanaians were 250 times more likely to be refused permission to enter the UK (Mactaggart and Gostin 1983). Indeed the United Kingdom Immigration Advisory Service also found that, on immigration statistics published for 1985, a New Zealander was 333 times more likely to be admitted to the UK than someone from Ghana.

Unemployment and housing

The publication, in 1977, of David Smith's report on *Racial Disadvantage in Britain* marked an important milestone in understanding the extent and nature of discriminatory behaviour against 'black' groups in this country. Smith's report provided evidence of the following points:

- As total unemployment rises, unemployment of minorities rises more steeply (p. 69).
- All minority groups had penetrated comparatively little into non-manual jobs (p. 73).
- The earnings of minority men are lower than those of white men (p. 84).
- Asians and West Indians tend to live in accommodation of a much lower quality, from a structural point of view, than that occupied by whites (p. 230).

Fifteen years later, unemployment among ethnic minorities was estimated at 22 per cent in 1993, compared with 10 per cent among white workers. Between the summers of 1992 and 1993 black unemployment rose 3 per cent but for whites it was 1 per cent. Among women the difference was even greater (*Guardian* 1994).

The media

In the realm of the media, several major studies appeared in the late 1970s and 1980s, studies that indicated the extent to which 'people have derived from the media a perception of the coloured population as a threat and a problem, a conception more conducive to the development of hostility towards them than acceptance' (Hartmann and Husband 1974: 208).

Troyna's (1981) later study of local media (newspaper and radio) also revealed that far more attention was paid by the press to the manifestations of racial conflict and tension than on the scarcity of social resources which underlie the reasons for this conflict.

Other aspects

Other research findings in this area are in the book by Skellington and Morris (1992). They cover the incidence of violence and harassment (physical and mental), social services and welfare benefits, housing, the criminal justice system, education and the labour market. Points such as the following are made:

- The number of racially motivated violent incidents in England and Wales in 1990 was 6,359 (p. 63).
- Blackness and poverty are more correlated than they were some years ago. The conditions of the black poor are deteriorating (p. 67).
- Various research studies reveal a higher incidence of diagnosis of schizophrenia among the black population compared with whites and suggest that black people tend to receive harsher forms of medication than equivalent white groups (p. 82).
- Discrimination is also revealed in the NHS employment practices, right through from consultant doctors to ancillary workers (p. 83).
- Evidence suggests that black minority ethnic groups are underrepresented as clients receiving the preventive and supportive elements of social services provision, but over-represented in those aspects of social services activity which involve social control functions and/or institutionalization (p. 87).
- Differential figures between blacks and whites were also revealed in studies on the legal system, in jury composition (p. 104), the magistracy (p. 105), solicitors and barristers (p. 106) and probation officers (p. 107).
- In 1989, the director of the Prison Reform Trust claimed that if white people were jailed at the same rate as black people, the total prison population of the UK would be 300,000. It is under 50,000 (p. 107).
- The incidence of school suspensions and expulsions was significantly higher for Afro-Caribbean pupils than others (p. 122).

Summing up

The climate, then, in which the contents of this book are set, is a profoundly complex one in terms of history, population complexity, political perspectives and a huge range of cultural identities. All this is further compounded by discrimination and racism. Both counsellors and clients are participants in this climate, and as such, are subject to the multitude of complex forces and attitudes that shape people's lives. The contents alone indicate that any overly simplistic assumptions about the nature of British society and the people who live within it just cannot be made. Counsellors and psychotherapists have to acknowledge that their assumptions and beliefs about and attitudes towards those who are culturally and racially different may well be, oversimplistic, judgemental and discriminatory. At worst and as a consequence, therapeutic aims may well have anti-therapeutic outcomes.

The context: the establishment of counselling and psychotherapy as healing systems in society today

'What she needs is a good listening to'
(From an advertisement on behalf of the National Society
for the Prevention of Cruelty to Children)

The previous section offered the reader an introduction to the complexity of today's multicultural society, a society that has also experienced in the last 20 to 30 years a substantial attitudinal shift towards the greater acceptance of counselling and psychotherapy.

A range of data is presented in the following pages charting this general development, a development that is leading towards a new professional helping infrastructure within society. As counselling becomes increasingly embedded in society the authors fear that it may at worst become like all other areas of intervention in people's lives, (mentioned in the previous pages): discriminatory and racist in practice. However, this is anticipating the contents of the final section of this chapter. Let us return to the situation of counselling today and chart some of its developments.

The development of counselling

The opening quotation above was used by the NSPCC in their advertising during the spring of 1994. Some years previously both the Midland Bank and the Labour Party coined the use of the term 'listening' within their slogans and advertising literature. The Labour Party thus became 'the listening party' and the Midland 'the listening bank'. It is suggested here that such advertising terminology was no accident but an attempt to create an ideological perspective based upon current recognizable trends in society.

Listening, of course, is a central activity in counselling and psychotherapy. So is empathy. As a technical concept that owes much of its origins to the development of the work of Dr Carl Rogers in client-centred therapy, over 20 different definitions have now been developed, including an extensive treatment of it by Rogers himself. Not lagging far behind, marketing personnel appended the term to a range of beauty products, including that of Empathy shampoo!

Similarly, at about the same time, a security company developed the slogan 'Securicor cares'. Care of others, in the general sense, is embodied within the concept of counselling. 'Care' also is a acronym for Rogers's core therapeutic conditions of counselling. CA stands for communicated authenticity (congruence, genuineness), R for regard (acceptance, warmth), and E for empathy.

However interesting, ironic and humorous the previous examples may be, they do give an indication of the impact of ideas derived from counselling and psychotherapy upon society during the last decade.

Certainly, a research survey conducted on behalf of the Royal College of Psychiatrists in 1991 revealed that 85 per cent of the 2,000 respondents believed that depression was caused by life events and that counselling, not medication, was the most appropriate form of assistance. Such a sizeable proportion again indicates the extent to which the public has adopted some of the belief systems of counsellors and psychotherapists themselves.

Significant landmarks

Of course, it is somewhat difficult to chart accurately the key points of this historical development of attitude change towards the talking therapies. However, some of the following will have provided contributory milestones on this journey.

The enormous influence of *Sigmund Freud*'s work. Though dating back to the turn of the century, the significance and impact of psychoanalysis and psychoanalytic thought upon this century has been very considerable indeed. Not only have these early ideas contributed to theories of personality and theories of therapy, they have permeated disciplines such as literature, art, philosophy, psychology, sociology, organizational development and many more. As a consequence, the ideas and concepts themselves have become part of everyday language, e.g. Freudian slips, the unconscious, the significance of dreams, defence mechanisms, projection, free association, the ego and so on. (A very readable account of Freud's work can be found in Jacobs 1992.)

The formation of the *National Marriage Guidance Council*. The Council first opened its doors in 1938, in response to the rising divorce figures at that time. The founder, Dr Herbert Gray, was convinced that relationships were under significant strain from the pressures of life in the twentieth century. As news of its work spread, the Council received many hundreds of requests from troubled couples and – from an earlier emphasis on research and education –

counselling emerged as the main service. A small London office opened in 1943, and in the ensuing five years, over 8,000 clients were seen.

By 1988 there were 160 centres offering almost a quarter of a million interviews per year. Sadly, marriages were still breaking down at the rate of 160,000 divorces per year and waiting lists to see a counsellor grew to almost 10,000, with queues of up to six months in the worst-affected areas.

Reorganized and relaunched in 1988 under the name Relate, (which embraced a commitment to all kinds of couple relationships) counsellors now work from a variety of community buildings, bringing the number of locations up to over 400 across the country.

Relate is a vigorous national organization often consulted by the media and is active in training over 400 counsellors a year and helps an average of 750 relationships every day (Relate 1992).

The Samaritans. The Samaritans were founded in 1953 by the Reverend Chad Varah, the first centre being run from the crypt of his church, St Stephen Wallbrook, in London. He responded to what he perceived to be a need for people to talk about things that may be unacceptable under normal circumstances, e.g. relationship problems, job worries, sexual difficulties, suicide, depression and so on.

The biggest branch of the Samaritans is in central London, though there are now over 200 branches throughout the UK. Some 2,500 volunteers take approximately 2.25 million phone calls per year. One example of a local branch (Sheffield) reveals that over 200 volunteers take about 24,000 phone calls each year.

The establishment of the *British Association for Counselling* (BAC). Formed in 1977, BAC grew out of the Standing Conference for the Advancement of Counselling, and was inaugurated in 1970 with the help of the National Council of Voluntary Organizations. In 1978 the headquarters moved from London to Rugby where it continues to base its operations.

Membership of the Association has grown from 1,300 in 1977 to 11,100 in 1994, a very substantial increase indeed. The aims of the Association are to:

- promote understanding of counselling
- increase availability of trained counsellors
- maintain and raise standards of training and practice
- provide support for counsellors and those using counselling skills
- respond to an increasing demand for information about counselling
- represent counselling at a national and international level
                    (British Association for Counselling 1987)

Increased training opportunities. The early 1970s saw the establishment of the first full-time courses of counselling training at London, Swansea and

Keele universities. Since then, formalized training courses, both full- and part-time, have mushroomed and are run by a wide range of organizations that include universities, colleges and independent training institutes.

The more recent explosion of *counselling literature*. This phenomenon has been most marked since about 1980. In addition to the publication of a substantial number of books on the subject, there has also been a wide range of newspaper articles, regular columns by therapists and articles written by clients themselves. Television and radio programmes have also proliferated in this time, often focusing upon causes of psychological distress and appropriate forms of treatment.

Development of theory. Running parallel to this wide-ranging development of interest has been the extraordinary development of theoretical perspectives for practitioners. Only a few years ago the number of 'brand name' therapies had risen to 481 in the United States alone! (Karasu et al. 1984).

Allied to, and as a consequence of the various factors depicted above, there has also been a significant expansion in the number of voluntary and statutory organizations offering counselling to the community. In addition specialist agencies concerned with mental health and minority groups have also emerged and developed. One example is: *Nafsiyat*, an intercultural therapy centre. Nafsiyat was set up in London in 1983 to provide a specialist psychotherapy service to black and other ethnic and cultural minorities (Kareem and Littlewood 1992: 14). The word 'Nafsiyat' was coined from three ancient languages, the syllables meaning mind, body and soul.

Jafar Kareem, an Indian trained in psychodynamic psychotherapy, conceived the idea of a specialist centre that would offer psychotherapy to black and ethnic minority people out of his experiences of working as a psychotherapist in the National Health Service. Concerned to offer a form of therapy that was relevant and pertinent to clients, Nafsiyat aimed to offer a form of dynamic psychotherapy which was not necessarily tied to one theoretical orientation but which derived its strength from various analytical, sociological and medical formulations. Kareem defined intercultural therapy as follows:

> A form of dynamic psychotherapy that takes into account the whole being of the patient – not only the individual concepts and constructs as presented to the therapist but also the patient's communal life experience in the world – both past and present. The very fact of being from another culture involves both conscious and unconscious assumptions, both in the patient and in the therapist. I believe that for the successful outcome of therapy it is essential to address these conscious and unconscious assumptions from the beginning.
>
> (Kareem 1978: 14)

The work of Nafsiyat in the UK has been considerable, not only in its development and delivery of intercultural therapy but also in its contributions to training and research in this field.

It seems as if these various influences outlined above have significantly affected, indeed confronted, the cultural stereotype so long prevalent in Britain of the 'stiff upper lip'. As 'talking about one's troubles' rather than burying such issues of concern has become much more acceptable, so too have opportunities developed for people to work in groups, either facilitator-led or self-help.

The above examples give an indication of the variety of ways in which the theoretical and therapeutic ideas originating at the turn of the century have had an enormous impact upon attitudes and responses to mental health issues in society today. In turn, these have influenced the development of a wide range of organizations offering counselling, in a variety of settings for both general use and specific disorders. Despite this considerable development, however, it is important to point out that a substantial proportion of counselling in Britain continues to be conducted in the voluntary sector, though an increasing number of posts are slowly being created in statutory and commercial organizations. Consideration is now being given to employing the services of counsellors from varying cultural/racial groups, thereby allowing more choice for people seeking counselling.

Squaring the circle

Tseng and Hsu (1979) have noted that four dominant modes of helping have always existed in all cultures. Putting it slightly differently, they note that the cultural modes of exploration and intervention in the area of personal distress proceed from the four reference points of supernatural intervention, social interaction, principles of nature and bodily functioning. See Figure 1.1 for a diagrammatic representation of this idea. Historically, in many societies, it is possible that the healers (wise elders, shamans, witch doctors, priests etc.) embodied all four modes depicted in Figure 1.2 in their healing powers. A healer, for example, may have listened to the troubled person's story (dialogue), appealed to the gods for help through prayer and ritual (spirituality), given the person berries or potions to take (medicinal) and finally recommended certain exercises or penance activities (behaviourism).

The sophisticated development of professional specialisms specifically in the last century has seen these particular helping activities develop into quite different and separate disciplines. Of course each form of helping depends on communication and dialogue. However, Freud warned as early as 1904 that communication and dialogue could not be left to chance (Jones 1959). The emergence of counselling, underpinned by research activity since the 1940s, has meant that considerable attention has been devoted to this particular

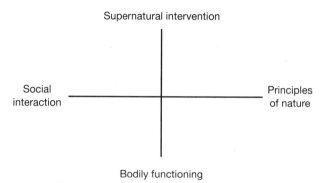

Figure 1.1   Four healing interventions

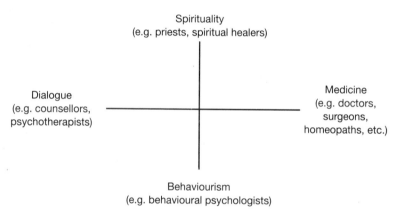

Figure 1.2   Four healing methods

aspect of human helping behaviour. As a result counsellors and psychotherapists have become more knowledgeable and specialized in this arena.

Doctors and priests have long enjoyed the established roles of helpers in the
community. The rather more recent advent of behaviourism and different
counselling approaches in this country has meant that there has been a
'squaring of the circle' of completing the spectrum of healing methods.
However, unlike traditional societies, each of these activities is now carried
out by different personnel using a wide variety of theoretical and practical
intervention styles to assist troubled people.

Notwithstanding the above variations, the dialogical approach of counselling and psychotherapy has now achieved some equivalency with other
approaches and acceptability with the public at large. This spread of interest,
supported by the huge increase in literature, training courses and media

exposure has led many allied professions, e.g. teaching, nursing, social work, etc. to adopt counselling skills as a vital component in their daily work. Counselling and psychotherapy has come of age.

The challenge

> Every worker in the mental health field should be trained to recognise the ways in which their own cultural upbringing is likely to have affected their perceptions of the problems which their clients bring . . .
>
> (Murphy 1986: 179)

This very pertinent quote effectively highlights one of the most important points emerging from this whole chapter. That is, the profound and often unconscious impact our own cultural heritage has upon our attitudes and perceptions towards others, especially those who are racially and culturally different to ourselves. One challenge that emerges from this, for counsellors, is that of their willingness and capacity to explore their cultural and racial origins in order to try to understand better their own cultural identity, beliefs and value systems. As part of this they also need to become more aware of their attitudes towards other groups and cultures, to become more aware of their stereotypes and their assumptions.

It could be argued that in its broadest sense all counselling is crosscultural in that it embodies two persons, who, by definition have already had differing backgrounds and thus, to a certain extent have their own unique identities (cultures). However, within the field of transcultural counselling, the potential differentness of the other (in terms of appearance, sound, dress, values etc.) will also have an impact upon the counsellor. Inevitably the counsellor will make assumptions in both scenarios. However, the assumptions made in transcultural counselling, as we shall see later, may have much more serious implications and consequences for the outcome.

Additionally, the counsellor requires an understanding of the political processes in society that continue to perpetuate racist and discriminatory processes. An understanding of these mechanisms is necessary in order for the counsellor, at the very least, to avoid recreating them within their therapeutic practice. Ideally, such knowledge will inform the counsellor's work and will contribute to informed, relevant and creative responses to the client and their concerns.

Contemporary critiques of counselling and psychotherapy have acknowledged that increasingly these professional activities have emphasized the nature of individual and personal pathology and isolated them from social and political concerns (Hillmann and Ventura 1992; Orbach 1993; Lago, C. 1994).

In summarizing the various perspectives above we believe that the challenge to counsellors is a multifaceted one:

- Do they understand the impact of their own past upon their assumptions about culture, identity, morals, etc.?
- Do they understand the discriminatory nature and power imbalance of the relationship between dominant and minority groups in society and how such practices are perpetuated?
- Can they enhance their own learning about the groups from which clients come?
- Are they open to a wide range of challenging and perhaps contradictory views of the world expressed by clients?
- How might their theories/models of counselling be extended or modified to incorporate a wider range of understanding and response modes to clients?
- How might their way of being with clients recognize and address the societal and political implications (as well as the emotional and psychological implications) of the client's situation?

> So I would see counsellors having a socially activist role in Britain as well, encouraging British society to look not only at what you are doing to yourselves . . . but what you are doing to other people in the world. British counsellors could benefit from being exposed to conditions in a developing country because of the stark and therefore . . . more visible tensions there, and this might help them to understand their own country better.
>
> (Swart, in Dryden 1990: 317)

2

Issues of race and power

> Given that relations between black and white groups over several centuries
> have been typified by oppression, exploitation and discrimination, how
> might contemporary relationships within counselling be transformed into
> creative (rather than further damaging) experiences?
>
> (Lago and Thompson 1989a: 208)

> What is evident, then is that racism is an ideology which is continually
> changing, being challenged, interrupted and reconstructed, and which
> often appears in contradictory forms. As such, its reproduction in schools,
> and elsewhere can be expected to be complex, multi-faceted and
> historically specific. . . . specific forms of racism can be expected to change,
> and inherited racist discourses are likely to be re-constituted. New
> circumstances are likely to lead to new formulations of racism.
>
> (Troyna 1993: 15)

Introduction

Counsellors are trained to work in a sensitive, skilled, and theoretically
informed manner with individuals seeking help. The process of their work is
dependent upon the quality of relationship that develops between them and
their clients. A considerable amount of time during their training, quite
appropriately, is devoted to understanding individual psychology and
pathology and the processes of healing through dialogue. They emerge thus
influenced from their training and then engage in counselling practice that
further reinforces their understanding of individual human beings. Their
primary focus becomes that of individuals and their pathologies and
difficulties.

The intention of this chapter, which we believe is central not only to this
text but to any counselling engagement, is that counsellors need also to have a
systematic structural understanding of society. Our contention is that racism,
for example, functions as a pathology of and in society. At worst a
counsellor's overconcentrated focus on individual pathology might deprive
them of important understandings of the client's world, understandings that
could be applied usefully in the counselling encounter.

We have previously asserted that:

(a) In order to understand relationships between black and white people today, a knowledge of the history between differing racial groups is required.
(b) Counsellors will also require an understanding of how contemporary society works in relation to race, the exercise of power, the effects of discrimination, stereotyping, how ideologies sabotage policies and so on. In short counsellors require a structural awareness of society.
(c) Counsellors require a personal awareness of where they stand in relation to these issues.

(Lago and Thompson 1989a: 207)

This chapter considers each of these aspects in turn.

Van Dijk (1993), in his multinational study of the racist discourse of elite groups in society, recognized that

> much elite text and talk about minorities may occasionally seem to express tolerance, understanding, acceptance or humanitarian world views, although such discourse is contradicted by a situation of structural inequality largely caused or condoned by these elites.

(p. 6)

A broad overview of those engaged in the counselling profession would reveal that many practitioners hold the various humanitarian world views referred to by Van Dijk (1993). Indeed, it would be somewhat alarming if counsellors did not espouse such philosophic concerns for their fellow beings, as they have often entered the profession as an expression of their own caring. However, we contend that, very much like the elite groups Van Dijk refers to above, counsellors are not necessarily aware of the nature or extent of the structural inequalities that so perjoratively affect black people's lives nor are clearly aware of their own position in those issues. Even if not actively involved in the various modes of oppression, their involvement in the problem of racism is characterized by unawareness, passivity, blind acceptance and indifference.

The profound effects of history on the rise of racism

> Her Majestie understanding that there are of late divers blackamoores brought into this realme, of which kinde of people there are allready here to manie . . . Her Majesty's pleasure therefore ys that those kinde of people should be sent forth of the lande . . .
> (From an open letter from Queen Elizabeth I sent on 11 July 1596 to mayors and sheriffs in different towns, quoted in Fryer 1984: 10)

In the first chapter we have already begun to describe the multiracial nature of British society. We referred to the historical perspective, offering brief data on when and why various groupings from other cultures and societies came to live in Britain. Popular memory often relates only to the so-called 'waves' of immigration that occurred in the 1960s.

Interestingly, Fryer (1984) points out that there were Africans in Britain before the English came here. They were soldiers in the Roman imperial army that occupied the southern part of Britain for 350 years. Among the troops defending Hadrian's Wall in the third century AD was a division of Moors. Fryer quotes other instances of African presence long before the sixteenth century, the time referred to in Chapter 1. In terms of continuous black presence, however, we have to date that from about the mid-sixteenth century.

Fryer's scholarly work provides an extraordinarily detailed and substantial account of the historical, political and social dimensions of Britain's relationship with black people over the last 500 years. Van Dijk (1993) talks about this period as a

> time when [European] elites have engaged in the predominant practice of derogation, inferiorization, exploitation, subjugation and occasional genocide of non-Europeans. These others were variously seen and treated as barbarians, savages, infidels, semi-animals, monsters, slaves, subordinates, 'niggers' (and related racist words), wetbacks, guest workers, insurgents, terrorists, economic refugees or many other categories combining the concept of threat, inferiority, alien origin, appearance and culture.
>
> (p. 52)

Our analysis draws heavily on Fryer's seminal work and readers are recommended to consult its extensive coverage of these issues.

The origins of racism in Britain are closely intertwined with the historical data recording early contacts between Britons and other (specifically black) cultures. The move from racial prejudice ('essentially irrational and . . . in large measure sub-conscious') towards racialism ('a rationalised ideology based upon what is purported to be irrefutable scientific fact') was portrayed by Charles Lyons (1975) in his review of black–white relations between 1530 and 1860.

The ancient myths of Africa and Africans, derived from travellers' tales, already held great sway in the sixteenth and seventeenth centuries. The formation and retention of racially prejudiced views is especially persistent, Fryer argues (1984: 153) in communities that are ethnically homogeneous, geographically isolated, technically backward or socially conservative, and where the knowledge and political power is concentrated in the hands of an elite. Such communities feel threatened by national or racial differences and their prejudices enhance group cohesion. England, in the sixteenth and seventeenth centuries was a classic instance of such a community, though its geographical isolation was rapidly being overcome and its technology was about to leap forward.

Racial prejudice is largely transmitted by word of mouth and is often 'scrappy and self-contradictory' (p. 134). Racism, by contrast, is transmitted largely through the written word and becomes relatively systematic, acquiring a pseudoscientific veneer that glosses over its irrationalities and enables it to claim intellectual respectability. The most important aspect of these distinctions, however, is the realization that the primary functions of race prejudice are cultural and psychological. The primary functions of racism, however, are economic and political.

This distinction was acutely observed and recorded by Morgan Godwyn in 1680 when he pointed out the economic basis and role of plantocracy racism. Fryer extracts the following five key points from the text of Godwyn's book:

1 Racist ideology was created by planters and slave merchants out of 'avarice'.
2 It was, initially, furtively spread.
3 Historically, by 1680, it had become respectable enough for its propagators in England to come into the open.
4 Opponents of racism were, as yet, few and uninfluential. There was little resistance.
5 One of the functions of racism was to justify the planters and merchants in their own eyes as well as in the eyes of society.

Finally Godwyn also proposed that the planters were prepared to say anything that would safeguard their profits. As Fryer points out, 'Godwyn was the first to analyse racism as a class ideology and even after 300 years neither his analysis nor his language has lost its cutting edge' (p. 148).

An extraordinary range of eighteenth- and nineteenth-century writers, famous for their contributions to liberalism, literature, philosophy and politics actually contributed significantly to the spread of racist views through their various writings. Such luminaries included: Sir William Petty, founder of modern political economy and one of the founders of the Royal Society (p. 151); John Locke, philosopher (p. 151); David Hume, philosopher (p. 152); William Knox, provost-marshal of the British colony of Georgia and author of religious tracts (p. 154); Edward Long, justice of the Vice-Admiralty Court and author of a history of Jamaica in 1774. 'Long's peculiar talent lay in linking a scientific-sounding assertion of black inferiority – he was the first pseudo-scientific racist – with a defence of black slavery . . .' (p. 157).

The above list, however, only provides a snapshot into contemporary thought in the eighteenth and nineteenth centuries. Indeed Charles Lawrence describes racism, by the 1770s, as being firmly established in Britain as a 'principal handmaiden of the slave trade and slavery' (foreword in Hammon and Jablow 1970).

Despite the end of the British slave trade in 1807 and slavery in 1833, racism was not then, and never has been since, dispensed with. Fryer notes that it was now too valuable as a component in the rise of the British empire. 'The culminating stage in the rise of English racism was the development of a strident pseudo-scientific mythology of race that would become the most important ingredient in British imperial theory' (Fryer 1984: 165).

The various government policies embodied in Britain's relationship with countries in its empire were dominated by racist perspectives, leading Fryer to conclude that 'the golden age of the British Empire was the golden age of British racism too' (p. 165).

We cannot even gain a sense of reassurance from the above accounts that racism was a minority and crazy view during this time. 'Virtually every scientist and intellectual in nineteenth-century Britain took it for granted that only people with white skin were capable of thinking and governing. . . . Only in the last 30 or 40 years has racism lost intellectual respectability' (p. 169).

Inevitably, a range of contending schools of pseudoscientific racist thought had developed over this period, but they were all agreed on one essential point: that black people were outsiders, that they should be forever barred from high office, from important posts in law and medicine in church and state and from having any important voice in their own affairs. Despite vigorous attempts in recent years in education, training and equal opportunities legislation to eradicate these attitudes, their existence in society is still highly prevalent as evidenced by a huge range of research studies demonstrating disadvantage and discrimination (Smith 1977; Skellington and Morris 1992).

An organic connection was also made in the nineteenth century between the attitude of the British ruling class to the peoples of its colonies and the attitude it took to the poor at home (p. 169). This interconnectedness of issues surrounding 'race' and 'class' has been much explored and debated in contemporary sociology. This very potent combination of factors embodied in the categories of race, class and economics continues to have a huge impact upon the relationships between groups of people in Britain today: between the rich and poor, employed and jobless, powerful and powerless, white and black, resident and immigrant, and so on. These issues are not just of passing concern to social scientists and therefore worth studying. They have a very real impact upon the direct, daily experience of black people's lives in Britain.

This section has attempted to capture, in just a few pages, the very serious, punitive and extensive range of attitudes, behaviours and practices that were formed over several centuries to justify inhuman, disrespectful and colonial domination of black peoples. Counsellors must take note of the impact such historical relations may have on any therapy relationships they develop in the present.

Towards a structural awareness: racism, power and powerlessness (definitions and practices)

For many white people who believe themselves to be tolerant, understanding, accepting and so on it is often very difficult to appreciate the multiplicity of mechanisms that exist in society which perpetuate systems of disadvantage among black people. As Troyna (1993) has so elegantly described in the opening quotation to this chapter, the ideology of racism is an immensely complex and changing phenomenon, and consequently racist practices become less visible, less specific and are therefore more difficult to notice and comprehend. The value of social science research outcomes in this field is that they show that, sadly, despite changes in legislation and working practices, the systems of disadvantage and racism continue.

Racism: definitions

Judy Katz (1978), in her very useful handbook for anti-racism training, provides the following definitions of racism:

1 A belief that human races have distinctive characteristics that determine their respective cultures, usually involving the idea that one's own race is superior and has the right to rule others.
2 A policy of enforcing such asserted rights.
3 A system of government and society based upon it. (*Random House Dictionary of the English Language* 1967)

To these definitions may be added:

4 Perpetuation of belief in the superiority of the White race.
5 Prejudice plus power.

(p. 51)

The final definition used above, though perhaps apparently simplistic, does contain a readily accessible formula for analysis of issues and events. If one views things from a prejudiced perspective and has the power to act out those views, the outcome is going to be racist.

An exercise to explore how racism works

Katz also includes in her book a training exercise that enables white people to explore the subtleties of those disadvantaging mechanisms within organizations. She invites participants to design a racist community (p. 46). The goals of the exercise are listed as: first, to identify the key elements of racism, and second, to discover how racism functions in our society.

Training groups are invited to brainstorm, on to flipchart paper, their design of a racist community or organization. Groups may wish to produce a community that is blatantly and overtly racist or one that is much more subtle.

The designs must take into account and define the various elements of any working community such as the following: the makeup and constitution of the community, identification of the decision-makers and how decisions are made, who controls the money, how formal and informal policies are created and so on.

After the designs have been created, the groups are invited to identify and discuss three major elements: first, the key elements of a racist community; second, a comparison of the designed community with real communities; and third, the issue that only whites have the power to oppress black people in this country and that black people do not have the power to oppress whites.

A racist counselling organization

This exercise can also be specifically applied to organizations. A counselling agency, designed according to these criteria, might look something like the following:

> **Name of organization:** 'We listen and we care'.
>
> **Aims of organization:** To provide counselling to anyone in the local community who requests it or is referred.
>
> **Organizational structure:**
>
> *Management committee.* This group was initially brought together by the present director (details below) who had tried for some years to get this organization off the ground. The management committee thus comprises local dignitaries chosen initially for their reputation of concern for people in the community combined with their positions of standing (e.g. town councillors, directors/employers of local companies, senior staff from allied projects/services, etc.). Both their concern and their access to sources of funding and other staffing provisions were criteria in their selection.
>
> *Director.* He is a highly qualified and experienced therapist. Having had a successful career in private practice in London (to which he had commuted) he had chosen to retire early! However, as a consequence of hearing about different local experiences and appreciating the lack of local counselling resources he initiated discussions which led to the eventual formation of the project. After funding and premises had been successfully located it was only a natural outcome that he was appointed as director of the project. He

negotiated a three-day contract only, as he did not wish to become embroiled in full-time work again.

Counsellors. There are two part-time paid counsellors and the remaining are voluntary. The part-time paid counsellors, because they are qualified and experienced, also provide in-house training and supervision to the volunteers. At present there are ten volunteers.

One of the part-time paid counsellors is a former trainee of the director. The other part-time colleague, appropriately professionally qualified, had worked in a similar project in another town before moving house to this locale.

The volunteer counsellors have been selected by a panel involving the director and the two part-time paid counsellors through interview. In some cases the candidates have been students on one of the local counselling courses and are thus already partially trained. The other candidates have been selected on their perceived sensitivity and receptivity to others, combined with their availability to attend the in-house training courses and provide voluntary provision.

Secretarial and reception staff. Reception is provided by a team of ten volunteers who work one afternoon or one evening per week. In most cases they have been located through 'friends of friends'. Most administrative and secretarial work is carried out by the director, who is assisted occasionally by a retired secretary who previously had been a personal assistant to the managing director of a local firm. (The managing director, incidentally, is on the management committee.)

Agency funding: Funding to pay the salaries, heating, lighting, rent and all other expenses is principally obtained from fund-raising efforts and grants from the local authority and trust funds. Clients are expected to pay a 'nominal contribution' set at a minimum of £5 per session, and where appropriate, in consultation with the counsellors, are invited to contribute more.

Decision-making/policy-setting: All major decisions and policies are created and set by the director in consultation with the Management committee. The two part-time counsellors meet the director weekly to monitor trends, discuss current issues and dilemmas and in general oversee the clinical work of the counselling team.

This brief description of an agency could, of course, be considerably expanded. However, there is enough material above for us to consider the implications of the question, 'What are the key elements that make this agency racist?' The specific racist implications are printed in brackets at the end of each of the following statements.

Name of organization: The name 'We listen and we care' obviously embodies important notions central to counselling. However, these philosophic sentiments can quickly break down in practice – for the wide variety of reasons detailed in this book.

Aims of organization: The statement is all-embracing and rather grand. However, as an ideology, what are the contradictions it conceals?

- Despite the open statement, patterns of client usage reveal that a disproportionate number of clients come from the area immediately surrounding the agency and the middle-class suburbs. Black clients are underrepresented, as compared with their population size in the town. (Is client usage monitored? How are actions taken to ensure that the agency is seen to cater for all?)
- Might this situation arise through a range of elements including directories of local resources, and who hears about the agency from the director's local talks? (Who initiates advertising? Where is it displayed? Where does the director give speeches?)
- How is the agency referred to, who refers clients, how can they self-refer, etc? (Referrals rely on the knowledge base and disposition of their referrers.)
- How welcoming to all clients is the service? (Receptionist behaviours and sensitivities can significantly affect the clientele of the service. Are there any black receptionists?)
- What is the effect of the locale in which the agency is located? (Its location will have effects upon usage.)

Organizational structure:

Management committee. This group comprises local dignitaries who already hold office in various commercial, civil and political organizations in the area. As a body,

- What is their racial composition?
- Are they fully sensitive to the needs of all elements of the local community?
- Their selection is subject to who the director knows and who they, themselves, might recommend. (Friends of friends and word of mouth are both restrictive mechanisms.)

Director. He received a very expensive analytic training many years before. Such training, inevitably, is only accessible, in the majority of cases, where candidates come from backgrounds of personal wealth and are acceptable to selection committees or training institutes. (Both these factors discriminate against the likelihood of black people attaining such life opportunities.) Also, having been the instigator of the idea of the project he automatically became its director after obtaining the funding. No other choice was considered. (This ensured that no other candidates were considered for the post, a denial of equal opportunity recruitment practice.)

Counsellors. One of the part-time counsellors had been a trainee of the director and thus this previous contact had clearly influenced the appointment. (Selection of people already in the system.) The other colleague had previous experience in a similar organization. (Previous experience, although in many cases helpful, also implies previous attitudes, unthinking acceptance of working practices gained from elsewhere and a closed response to new challenges.)

The volunteer counsellors have variously been students of the senior counsellors. (They have trained in the same mould and are already schooled in the subtle power relationships of student/teacher which is then replicated in the paid/voluntary skilled/less skilled division of labour in the agency. Inevitably these elements lead to restrictive styles of counselling practice and a perpetuation of the status quo of previous power differentials.)

Reception staff. They have been located predominantly through a system of friends of friends. (Who knows who? Who is considered OK? How are such criteria decided? What are the grounds for selection?)

Client fees: Could these be paid by all clients? (On what criteria do the counsellors decide how much the clients should pay? Are these criteria set by agency policy etc?)

Decision-making/policy-setting: Within the practices of how decisions and policies are made within the agency, how do the whole gamut of issues relating to service delivery to minority groups become considered and acted upon?

Brief summary

The inclusivity of the above processes ensure, through no malign intention, that certain issues are seldom, if ever, taken into account within certain organizations. Consequently many of the questions relating to any discriminatory practice might never be considered. In addition if the ideology of the agency is that 'we counsel all', how dare it be challenged about biased delivery?

As we may see from the above, discriminatory processes operate at ideological, organizational and personal levels. Perhaps one criteria for the judgement of health of any organization is its capacity to receive criticism, to reflect upon its operating mechanisms and then to amend these appropriately in the light of the evidence gathered.

The dynamics of the white counsellor/black client counselling partnership

In our chapter on 'Counselling and race' (Lago and Thompson 1989a) we developed a matrix of counselling pairings, as indicated in Figure 2.1.

| White client | White counsellor |
Black counsellor	Black client
White client	Black counsellor
White counsellor	Black client

Figure 2.1   Matrix of counsellor dyads

This diagram then acted as a base for exploration of the different issues, elements and dynamics potentially present in each of the above pairings. However, we will concentrate here on the white counsellor/black client interactions. In that chapter we wrote the following:

> A series of questions can assist us in addressing, briefly the issues for a white counsellor with a black client: how structurally aware of society is the counsellor?; do they have an understanding of the myriad of disadvantaging mechanisms that exist in contemporary society in relation to black people?; what class background are they from?; what experience of black people have they had?; and what effects, perceptions, and attitudes have these left upon the counsellor?
>
> (p. 211)

From experience gained by the authors whilst involved in training groups, it seems reasonable to state that many white people are quite unable to cope with radical black-perspectives and black people's pain and anger, specifically in relation to racism. Rogers (1969) has noted this phenomenon and suggests that white people who are effective in responding to oppressed groups seem to learn two attitudes. One is the realization and ownership of the fact that 'I think white'. The other is the ability to respond empathically, to be able to enter into the black person's world of hate, bitterness, and resentment, and to know that world as an understandable, acceptable part of reality. To achieve this ability Rogers suggests that the white persons themselves need to listen to their own feelings of anger at unjust situations. This is clearly something that could most usefully be done in training and therapy, in order that the fullest opportunities for personal learning may be gained.

> From the perspective of power, this combination of white counsellor with black client has a potential danger, namely a perpetuation of the notion of white superiority. The white person, as the counsellor in this situation, has the power. The sensitive handling of that power is absolutely crucial. For example, white counsellors have to work out ways of enhancing their own sensitivity and knowledge of client groups beyond the counselling framework. The pursuit of this knowledge, however justified that might be within the counselling process, could be perceived as an unethical abuse of their power. Black clients so used would have every right to experience further anger and a sense of injustice.
>
> (Lago and Thompson 1989a: 211–12)

These various aspects all relate to the potential complexity of any relationship between black and white people. At worst it is a relationship overloaded, burdened and profoundly affected by the past, generally speaking, and by the past lives of the two people engaging in the counselling relationship specifically.

To add to the seriousness and weight of the above, Carotenuto reminds us of the very inequality of power inherent in any therapeutic relationship. He says:

> however often we tend to conceal the fact that no other profession involves a greater inequality of power than the psychotherapists' in which one of the two poles is always, by definition, psychologically weaker than the other. For reasons intrinsic and structural to the psychological field, when a person is overwhelmed by suffering or convinced that his/her rational dimension, which up to that moment had qualified them as a human being, has failed, asks someone stronger than them to save them, then he/she places that person in a position of power and superiority. This could also be why we undertake this profession; it is the only one that allows us to deal always with weaker individuals, in partial indentification with the omnipotent figure of saviour offering a hand to the suffering.
>
> (Carotenuto 1992: 51)

This final quote on the power imbalance in therapy, combined with the various historical origins and contemporary mechanisms of racism described earlier in the chapter, serves to confront all therapists with the immensely delicate task transcultural counselling poses. Counsellors need to be acutely aware of these issues and where they stand in relation to them, both as persons in society and as therapists.

— 3

Towards understanding culture

An individual cannot, through introspection and self-examination, understand himself or the forces that mould his life, without understanding his culture.

(Thomas and Sillen 1972, frontispiece)

Culture: a complex word

Culture is one of the two or three most complicated words in the English language.

This quote, to be found in Raymond Williams's book *Keywords* (1983: 87), not only tells us something about the importance of the word but also hints at the multiplicity of its definitions and its manifestations. It has been estimated that, by the early 1960s, there were in excess of 160 different definitions of culture in the social science literature!

Williams devotes six pages of his book to this keyword 'culture'. Incidentally, a further three pages are given over to the word 'racial'. This factor alone, we believe, indicates the potential magnitude of the task not only that we took on in writing this book but which also faces any counsellor embarking upon a process of counselling with someone who is culturally or racially different. The words themselves ('culture', 'racial') have immense realms of meaning and diverse usages in history. As 'culture' is one of three keywords in the title of this book it seems appropriate to outline some of its historical usages, implications and connotations and then move towards an explicit statement of how we see this concept. There is no doubt that – perhaps as a reflection of the huge number of academic definitions mentioned above – we all probably have slightly different understandings and thus uses of the word. Though this range of usage can offer subtlety and complexity of meaning it can also create immense misunderstanding.

Following on from the quote given above, Williams continues his enquiry into the complexity of culture:

This is so partly because of its intricate historical development, in several European languages, but mainly because it has now come to be used for important concepts in several distinct intellectual disciplines and in several distinct and incompatible systems of thought.

(Williams 1983: 87)

Having Latin origins, the ultimate traceable word 'colere' had a range of meanings: inhabit, cultivate, protect, honour with worship. By the early fifteenth century, the word 'culture' had passed into English with primary meanings in husbandry, the tending of natural growth.

Williams goes on to say that 'culture, in all its early uses was a noun of process: the tending of something, basically crops and animals' (p. 87). Through a slightly different linguistic route, by a century later, the term had developed an important next stage of meaning, by metaphor, and was extended to the process of human development.

'Culture', as an independent noun was not important, according to Williams, before the late eighteenth and early nineteenth centuries.

Connotative, metaphorical and linked terms such as 'civility', 'cultivation' and 'cultivated' were all being developed at this time, thus laying a basis for some of the modern complexities referred to earlier.

The developments associated with 'culture' in the French and German languages also have to be recognized. The term *couture*, the original French name for culture, has obviously since developed its own very specialized meanings in the world of fashion, Williams argues. In France, 'culture' became linked to the noun 'civilisation' by the mid-eighteenth century (p. 89). In German, the term *cultur* (late eighteenth century) and later *kultur* (nineteenth century) was mainly used as a synonym (as in the French) for civilization, first in the abstract sense of a general process of becoming civilized or cultivated; second, in the sense established by eighteenth-century universal historians, as a description of the secular process of human development.

There was then a decisive change of use in Herder. In his unfinished *Ideas on the Philosophy of the History of Mankind*, written between 1784 and 1791, he wrote of *cultur*: 'nothing is more indeterminate than this word, and nothing more deceptive than its application to all nations and periods' (quoted in Williams 1983: 89).

He attacked the assumption of the universal histories that 'civilization' or 'culture', the historical self-development of humanity, was what we would now call a unilinear process, leading to the high and dominant point of eighteenth-century culture. Indeed he attacked what he called European subjugation and domination of the four quarters of the globe, and wrote:

men of all the quarters of the globe, who have perished over the ages, you have not lived solely to manure the earth with your ashes, so that at the end of time your prosperity should be made happy by European culture. The very thought of a superior European culture is a blatant insult to the majesty of Nature.

(quoted in Williams 1983: 89)

The very radical tone of the above quote, written some 200 years ago, contains philosophic values that are certainly implied and indeed made explicit in other parts of this book. For example, it expresses the belief that cultures are different *not* deficient. All cultures are sufficient unto themselves. Also, it confronts the false superiority assumed in much of western colonial thinking and practices, a false superiority and prejudice that has its historical roots in phenomena such as the triangular slave trade and the colonialization of other countries.

Originally influenced by G.F. Klemm's *General Cultural History of Mankind*, written in Germany between 1843 and 1852 (see Williams 1983: 90), which traced human development from savagery through domestication to freedom, the work of an American anthropologist, Morgan (reported by Williams 1983), traces comparable stages commencing with ancient society and culminating in civilization. This was directly followed in England by Tyler in *Primitive Culture* (1903). It is along this line of reference that the dominant sense of the word in modern social sciences has to be traced. Along the way the term 'folk culture' had become introduced as a way of emphasizing national and traditional cultures. It was also used at this time to distinguish between things human and the mechanical, inhuman, abstract and related concepts emerging out of industrial development.

We can easily define now, Williams writes (1983: 90), the sense which depends on a literal continuity of physical process – as in 'sugar beet culture' or, in the specialized physical application in bacteriology since the 1880s, 'germ culture'. However, once this physical definition has been identified, three broad active categories of usage have to be recognized. They are: first, the independent and abstract noun which describes a general process of intellectual, spiritual and aesthetic development from the eighteenth century; second, the independent noun whether used generally or specifically, which indicates a particular way of life, whether of a people, a period, a group, or humanity in general; third, the independent and abstract noun which describes the works and practices of intellectual, especially artistic, activity. This can often be one of the most widespread uses of the term – culture as music, literature, painting, sculpture, theatre and films – though, in fact, this usage is a relatively late addition.

This variety of usages and connotative meanings indicates a complex argument about not only the relations between general human development and a particular way of life, but also between both of these and the works and practices of art and intelligence (p. 91.) A classic difference apparently exists between the disciplines of archaeology and cultural anthropology – when reference to culture is primarily to material production – while in history and cultural studies the reference is primarily to signifying or symbolic systems.

Williams continues:

The anthropological use is common in the German, Scandinavian and Slavonic language groups, but it is distinctly subordinate to the senses of art and learning, or of a general process of human development in Italian and French. Between languages as within a language, the range and complexity of sense and reference indicate both difference of intellectual position and some blurring or overlapping. These variations, of whatever kind, necessarily involve alternative views of the activities, relationships and processes which this complex word indicates. The complexity is not finally in the word but in the problems which its variations of use significantly indicate.

(p. 91)

The above passages represent our attempt to précis Raymond Williams's extended considerations of the word 'culture'. We can begin to see what a potent and difficult concept it is that we are touching upon when we simply refer to the word 'culture'. And yet, with all of these meanings, Williams provides us with further 'stings in the tail' by noting other developments of the term – e.g. culture-vulture, cultural (adjectival use becoming common in the 1890s), sub-culture, culturalism, etc. – and also acknowledging how the term has attracted hostility in English. 'It is significant that virtually all the hostility has been connected with uses involving claims to superior knowledge' (p. 92).

Interestingly, in their chapter on 'The scope and methods of cross-cultural research', Frijda and Johoda chose to avoid the task of defining culture: 'Like most psychologists we are not anxious to dispel the illusion . . . that we know what we mean by this concept' (Frijda and Johoda 1969).

Unlike Frijda and Johoda, we will attempt to offer some operational definitions that we hope will inform our usage of the term in this book.

Culture: some further thoughts and working definitions

Geert Hofstede, an international management consultant, has defined culture as 'the collective mental programming of a people in an environment' (1980). In short, it applies to every facet of behaviour, interpersonal relations, ways of thinking, feeling, speaking and so on. This definition, then, does not relate simply either to the artefacts of culture (that might include such items as music, art and architectural designs) or to its usage as a term inferring deficiency, but rather is focused directly on how people understand how they should live and behave within their own grouping.

When we think of culture in relation to people's behaviour, there is a great temptation to consider exotic or foreign cultures. We often fail to see ourselves as being products of cultures, of our upbringing and our locale. We can so easily assume the stance of apparently neutral outside observers, judging quite coolly and at a distance what others do and how they do it!

For example, in considering greetings behaviour, what do you think when observing men greeting each other by kissing on both cheeks as opposed to shaking hands? Or how might you react if someone, in being introduced to you, bowed from a distance when you might have expected a handshake or kiss?

We might have a whole myriad of reactions, but it is important to acknowledge that these very reactions are programmed by our own culturally determined views of the world. We cannot but judge others upon the criteria that we hold to be true, polite and appropriate. Consequently, in any transcultural counselling encounter a situation develops in which two people may be judging each other by two sets of quite different criteria. Further, it is likely that both parties will not recognize this and even if they did, would not satisfactorily be able to articulate why it was that they behaved how they had!

Ruth Benedict (1968) has examined the arbitrary nature of culture and notes that all over the world, since the beginning of human history, it can be shown that people have been able to adopt the cultures of others. She states that there is nothing in the biological structure of people that makes this process difficult. People are not committed in detail by their biological constitution to any particular variety of behaviours. The great diversity of social solutions that people have worked out in different cultures are all equally possible on the basis of their original endowment. She thus asserts that culture is not a biologically transmitted complex. By implication, then, it is a socially transmitted one.

Responding to the inner or the outer?

The point has already been made that in any encounter between two visibly different persons, one judges the other based upon personal criteria which are pre-established and in some part stimulated by how the other person looks and behaves. Refining this somewhat further and based on Benedict's findings above, let us consider a counselling session where a white therapist is consulted by a black client. At worst, the white therapist might respond, in all sorts of ways to the visibility of difference, the black skin, failing completely to recognize the inner 'being' of the client that may be profoundly rooted in the same culture as the therapist. Only difference will be seen, the similarity of culture perhaps going unrecognized.

Of course, this is one of several key issues that are being addressed in this book. The above paragraph presents this issue very starkly. The lived experience of counselling interviews is considerably more complex than this, though at worst, the outcome might rest upon this initial impact of visibility of difference.

An analogy with the wider world of counselling is pertinent here. Counsellors are trained to listen to their clients and to respond to what it is they hear and sense of the client's inner world. Trained counsellors become sensitive to the fact that what clients present (indeed what we all most often present to the outside world) are their defence systems. What we see, therefore, from the outside, are manifestations of people's defence systems. If counsellors can suspend their judgements of what they see and instead, attend to what they hear and what the client has to say about their inner world, they come closer to understanding the person inside the bodily mask they are seeing. Counsellors and therapists are trained and sensitized to this purpose. Notwithstanding all of this, however, all human beings – counsellors included – do respond to and judge others, initially, on the basis of their own prejudices. This first point of contact, then, between culturally and racially different counselling pairings is profoundly crucial and will impact upon what might ensue between the two persons and whether the process will be deemed to have been therapeutically useful.

Culture and the individual

We have recognized above that culture is socially transmitted and profoundly affects our ways of seeing and thinking about the world, of understanding relationships among people, things and events, of establishing preferences and purposes, and of carrying out actions and pursuing goals.

From a sociological perspective, Bourdieu (1976) describes culture as not merely being a common code or even a common catalogue of answers to recurring problems; he asserts that it is a

> common set of previously assimilated master plans from which, by an act of invention, similar to that involved in the writing of music, an infinite number of individual patterns directly applicable to specific situations are generated.
>
> (Bourdieu 1976: 194)

Later in the same chapter Bourdieu investigates the role of social institutions (in this case the school) in establishing masterplans of thought in consciousness and in transmitting the (cultural) unconscious, thus producing individuals equipped with the unconscious system (or deeply buried) masterplan that constitutes their culture.

Bourdieu's phrase, 'an act of invention', could apply to acts of behaviour within a situation. That act of behaviour, depending upon the person, could conceivably be one from within a very wide range of potential behaviours culturally acceptable (or not) for that situation. The choice of that behaviour is likely to be the result of the complex factors that constitute the cultural background and the personality of the actor, as Yeaxlee (1925) reminds us: the personality 'is not static but dynamic . . . it is perpetually receptive and creative'.

For many years this realization has remained a fundamental problem for the disciplines of psychology and sociology: the relation between the individual and the social order. Ruth Benedict (1968) writes that

> no culture yet observed has been able to eradicate the differences in the temperaments of the persons who compose it. It is always a give-and-take.
> The problem of the individual is not clarified by stressing the antagonism between culture and the individual, but by stressing their mutual reinforcement. This rapport is so close that it is not possible to discuss patterns of culture without considering specifically their relations to individual psychology.
>
> (Benedict 1968: 183)

This realization is important and takes us beyond the findings of Kardiner (1947, 1959) and Linton (1945) who, in an extensive joint study reflecting anthropological and psychoanalytic origins, convincingly demonstrated that each culture tends to create and is supported by a 'basic personality type' composed of the complex personality characteristics that are congenial to the total range of institutions within a given culture.

This development, then, of the complex relationship between individual personality and culture further complicates the dynamics of any transcultural counselling partnership. The dynamic interplay between the two factors (personality and culture) which is manifested in all people's behaviour removes any possibility for simplistic predictions of other's behaviour and any assumptions about what they believe, think, what their guiding constructs are, and so on.

It has been our experience that there are situations in which, with clients having profoundly different cultural origins to ourselves, nevertheless a process of counselling has been helpful. Our hypothesis, in these circumstances, is that the personality traits within the clients have been open and conducive to our counselling style and approach. Despite the enormous cultural gulf, and all the differences that implies, successful therapeutic work has occurred.

Cultural understanding: the demands on the counsellor

> White culture is such a dominant norm that it acts as an invisible veil that prevents people from seeing counselling as a potentially biased system.
>
> (Katz 1985: in 615–24)

This chapter, so far, has concentrated upon an extended discussion of the term 'culture' and continued with offering several definitions that are operationally consistent with the way in which the notion, culture, is being used in this text. Culture profoundly affects people's ways of being, their behaviour, their interpersonal relationships, their notions of meaning and so on.

Valentine's (1968) definition of culture requires any outsider, in our case, the counsellor – to understand that 'the culture of a particular people or other social body is everything one must learn in order to behave in ways that are recognizable, predictable and understandable to those people'.

Valentine's statement throws down a considerable challenge. She says 'everything one must learn'. How does the counsellor learn?

By listening to the client? Self-evidently this represents a therapist's core activity. However, in listening, what is heard will be the presentation of the dilemma or problem currently being experienced by the client, mediated through their personality type and style influenced by their cultural origins. Only tangentially, therefore, might the counsellor gather a cultural understanding of the client.

By attending to the client's behaviour? If the client scratches their nose or constantly stares at the counsellor, for example, are they behaving culturally appropriately, or personally reacting to the stress of the environment or simply responding to physiological demands at this time (their nose itches or they may be concentrating)? Again, the counsellor may only have intuitions of cultural phenomena affecting the client, and indeed these intuitions may be quite inaccurate.

By asking the client? If you, as client, were asked about your culture, what would you say? How would you describe it, what aspects would you concentrate upon? Any description you gave would be partial and extremely limited. Also, such questions from the counsellor could indicate to you as client that the counsellor is really concerned to understand and help you. However, such questions could cause you to resent their inquisitiveness and curiosity or leave you feeling that the counsellor was more interested in your culture, your differentness, than in you and the difficulties you are currently facing. Emotionally, your response might be one of mistrust of motive and possible withdrawal from the counselling. An underlying fear, sometimes expressed by members of minority groups, is that 'the counsellor only wants to know because they want to find out about us, and I am aware there are many occasions, historically, where such knowledge has been used against me or my forebears.'

Asking, then, though apparently the most obvious strategy, might have considerable implications upon the client's perception and trust of the counsellor and will not necessarily yield the information the counsellor feels they require.

By consulting other sources of information? These might be through books, films, attending training courses and through conversations with other people. These demands certainly put pressures on counsellors to engage in a considerable amount of extra work outside their counselling activity. Given the huge number and variety of cultures in Britain alone, it would be impossible for any counsellor to accumulate such knowledge. A more realistic perspective might be for the counsellor to try to begin to get to know something of those specific cultures from which their clients most regularly come.

This whole section advocates that the counsellor needs to be culturally informed. However, the responses to each question above on how might the counsellor know more, pose further complexities.

One training mechanism developed in the United States to fulfil such purposes is called a 'culturegram'.[1] This is a regularly updated, written description about three pages in length, offering details of some principle characteristics of a culture. The organization that produces them has culturegrams now for a huge range of cultures in the world. Such sources of information might be useful, for example, to a student counsellor seeing many international students from certain countries or to a counsellor who works with recently arrived refugees. In these cases, where the counsellor and client come from distinctly different cultures, appropriate information exists in this readily accessible form.

However there are quite distinct limits on the precise nature and interpretation of this information. It could be argued that what is written reflects more the position of the (culturally different) author rather than the culture described. Phenomena described from an outsider's cultural perspective may be understood quite differently from within the insider's frame of reference. Also, though perhaps broad cultural tendencies may be describable, the extent to which they are acceptable as truth and therefore applicable to the complete range of personalities within that culture has to be seriously questioned.

Any descriptions of another culture will always be limited. It is certainly likely that such descriptions would not encompass the range of data that significantly affects different aspects of interpersonal behaviour featured in the next chapter. The counsellor will still be short of information that they consider might be useful to them, i.e. insights into how the client's cultural upbringing may affect their expectations of, and behaviour in, the counselling relationship.

What also has to be faced here is the (false) expectation that if we come to know something then that will automatically inform or help us modify our behaviour. Even if I know that your pattern of eye contact is culturally determined and does not signify what I interpret it to mean, I will still find it hard, if not impossible, to suspend my judgements about it and allow for it or modify my own behaviour to respond to it. Knowing and behaving are not necessarily easily linked.

If we return to Valentine's quote, she asserts that the learning has to occur in order to behave in ways that are 'recognizable, predictable and understandable to [others]'. Certainly, when people share cultural origins and understandings, they share, often without any awareness, sufficient 'recipes' for understanding each other's present behaviour and predicting their future behaviour.

Reversing Valentine's statement somewhat, could we engage in a process of learning about our own cultural selves sufficiently to understand, recognize and predict our own behaviours? This realm of self-understanding might also then give us insights into others' cultural positions through our empathy and through our imagination. Even here, in this venture, we are likely to be considerably challenged. Viewed from an outside perspective, Scheutz (1944) suggests that 'all cultural knowledge and practices are incoherent, only partially clear and not at all free from contradictions'. This statement has two implications. First, when we view others' cultures we may have the (perhaps uncomfortable) experience of trying to understand phenomena that are not at all clear or straightforward. Second, when we examine our own, we may not even appreciate the incoherences and contradictions that exist unless we are assisted by the help of cultural outsiders.

In summation, this last section of the chapter has explored the immense realms of difficulty likely to be experienced in trying to move towards a greater cultural understanding of ourselves and of others. A range of methods for attaining this knowledge have been suggested though each, on their own, will not be satisfactory in generating the range, depth and subtlety of understanding that we believe is required to be successful in any counselling ventures with culturally different clients.

Note

1 Culturegrams are produced by the David M. Kennedy Center for International Studies, Brigham Young University, 280 Harald R. Clark Building, Pravo, Utah 84602, USA.

Cultural barriers to communication

> People carry culture with them. When they leave one group setting for another they do not shed its cultural premises.
>
> (Becker and Gear 1960)

> We are all culturally conditioned. We see the world in the way we have learned to see it. Only to a limited extent can we, in our thinking, step out of the boundaries imposed by our cultural conditioning.
>
> (Hofstede 1980)

Introduction

Having discussed the complexity of culture in the previous chapter, the intention here is to offer ideas on the huge range of cultural differences that can be present when two people meet in the counselling setting.

The process of counselling is quintessentially based upon sensitive, understanding and accurate communication between counsellor and client. The point was made in Chapter 1 that counselling research has led the way in highlighting specific skills and styles of being that can lead to optimal outcomes for clients.

While communication constitutes part of the visible and audible aspects of people's behaviour, the inner origins of such messages come from the complex inner workings of our minds, our emotions, our memories, our relationships and so on. This book encourages counsellors to understand more fully their inner complexities and, specifically, their own cultural barriers to communication.

This chapter moves from an account of a training exercise – that provides a range of ideas generated by many participants on courses – to offering three different perspectives of differences between cultures: the work of E.T. Hall, the work of G. Hofstede, and the iceberg conception of culture. Inevitably, not all theoretical perspectives or indeed cultural differences are listed here. However, the views that are offered provide a resounding range of ideas and phenomena, sufficient to make us dwell deeply on the following question: with so many potential and actual differences between us, will we ever be able to communicate satisfactorily – has transcultural counselling any chance whatsoever?

A training exercise

The authors have often used the following training exercise as a way of helping groups think more about what cultural barriers to communication might be. Two stick figures having been drawn on the board, the group is invited to brainstorm as many cultural barriers to communication that they can think of existing between any two people who come from differing cultures. In quite a short time, an amazing array of ideas can be presented. Initially, the exercise is introduced in terms of the general barriers to communication any two people would experience.

A further development is to consider that the two figures, described as being culturally and racially different to each other, are a counsellor/client dyad. This secondary brainstorm can then produce further specialized ideas relating to cultural barriers affecting the counselling process.

Figure 4.1 very quickly provides us with a huge range of issues that are potentially present in any meeting between two people who are culturally and racially different. The complexity of this situation is further realized when one takes into account that person A, already having all these aspects, attitudes and attributes is trying to communicate with person B, also possessing these aspects, though differently constituted. Each is different to the other. Each also then proceeds to see, perceive, attribute and project on to the other from their own understanding of the world. Let us illuminate this with an example.

Person A is tall. She comes from a society of tall people and is thus used to conversations with others of a similar height. However, when confronted with person B, a shorter person, she has to significantly change her posture to communicate. The change in posture thus affects her attitude towards the other person as it reminds her of sayings she heard in her childhood about never trusting shorter people.

Thus person A, within her own culture, is fine. On meeting person B, she develops a set of reactions based upon her own culturally determined system of interpretation. Likewise person B, from their perspective, perceives the tallness of person A as potentially threatening and becomes fearful of her potential power. This leads B into being somewhat timid and withdrawn in A's company.

A perceives B
A judges B on A's system of categorizing people
A's behaviour and communication is thus likely to be affected.

B perceives A
B judges A on B's system of categorizing people
B's behaviour and communication is thus likely to be affected.

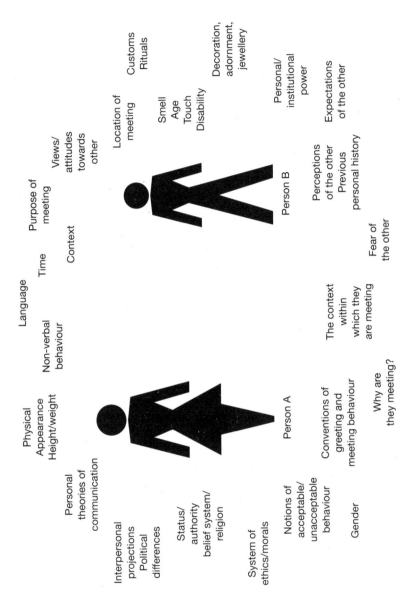

Figure 4.1 Cultural barriers to communication

This apparently very simple example of just one difference, of relative tallness, offers an insight into the potential complexity of the impact of difference upon communication. If the two persons were to be meeting for counselling, the scenario presented above indicates that whoever was counsellor, their capacity to be accepting of and non-judgemental towards the other, as client, is already limited. This demonstrates that the counsellor may have considerable difficulty in fully offering one of the core therapeutic conditions as defined by Rogers (1987) for successful therapy to occur, that of acceptance or non-judgementalism.

The work of Edward T. Hall

Edward Hall has written a series of books which are concerned to stimulate the view that in addition to learning other's languages we must also grasp the need for what he calls 'cultural literacy'. Broadly speaking, this is the ability to be sensitive to, and understanding of, the ways of being that are determined by different cultures.

For example, Triandis (1975) relates how an American visitor asked his Greek acquaintance what time they should come to his house for dinner. The Greek villager replied 'anytime'. Now in American usage, apparently, the expression 'anytime' is a non-invitation that people give to appear polite but which they hope will not lead to anything. The Greek, however, actually meant that the American would be welcome any time, because in Greek culture, putting limits on when a guest can come is deemed insulting (Furnham and Bochner 1986: 206). The consequences of such misunderstandings can lead to the attribution of negative values upon the other person and inevitably contribute towards a deterioration of the relationship. Edward Hall's books are full of anecdotal accounts from all over the world of such breakdowns in communication. Based on this wide experience and knowledge of differences between cultures, he has attempted to construct a set of hypotheses on how cultures differ (Hall 1959, 1966, 1976a and 1983).

He proposes five major categories of difference between cultures. These propositions are supported by considerable research literature. The categories are space, time, verbal behaviour, non-verbal behaviour and context. These are detailed below.

Space (proxemics)

People's feelings about being properly oriented in space runs deep . . . such knowledge is ultimately linked to survival and sanity. To be disoriented in space is to be psychotic.

(Hall 1966)

Edward Hall subdivides this category on space into five subsections:

Interpersonal space

Cultures have different conventions about the space between individuals in social situations. For example, people from certain cultures stand and converse at much closer distances than British people. Feelings of discomfort can soon be generated in such circumstances by the person who feels their space is being 'intruded'. However, they are often not fully aware of why they are experiencing such discomfort!

Olfactory space

Cultures have different ways of using the sense of smell. In Middle Eastern countries it can be a way of sensing the other person, whereas in Britain, perfumes and talcum powders are used to screen out natural smells.

Thermal space

The experience of space can be sensed through thermal sensations, e.g. 'feeling hot under the collar' or blushing.

Visual space

We use space visually to gather and convey information.

Sociofugal and sociopetal space

These terms relate to the different ways in which cultures use furniture arrangements and room designs, for example, that either enhance or inhibit interactions between people.

Time

Hall divides time into two broad categories, monochronic and polychronic.

Monochronic time

This refers, in general terms, to the increasingly dominant world view of the 24-hour day in which only that time system for measurement exists, e.g. 'The train leaves at 9.35 a.m' or 'Come to dinner at 8.00 p.m.'

Polychronic time

This is a much less well-known view of time but is practised by certain cultures. Hall cites the example of the Hopi Indians in the United States who have a belief in each thing, each person as having their own time. This concept is therefore very rooted in an individual's own experiencing.

Beyond those broad divisions, we are also informed of subdivisions of monochronic time that could have enormous implications for the relationships between counsellors and culturally different clients.

Appointment times   If the counsellor sets the appointment for 7.00 p.m., does the client turn up ten minutes before, or 'on the dot', or an hour later? Different cultures have different expectations and practices. 7.00 p.m. does not necessarily mean 7.00 p.m. exactly as determined by monochronic time. Cultural time modifies the precise time indicated, adding or subtracting so much time as is culturally understood and agreed.

Acquaintance time   This is the time considered polite in which to establish acquaintanceship before moving on to the matter that is the purpose of the meeting. This convention might have considerable implications for the counsellor in terms of their behaviour in the early part of an interview.

Discussion time   In business meetings, who is involved, who takes the decisions, how can decisions be taken and when? If we transpose Hall's conception of business meetings into counselling sessions, there are implications as to who makes decisions, the counsellor or the client, and who else is or should be involved in the process (e.g. family and friends, etc.).

Visiting time   How long meetings or social gatherings last is also determined culturally. The counsellor, within their interview rooms, might offer 50-minute sessions. If they were to visit a client in their own accommodation it might be considered more appropriate for the client to determine (culturally) how long they should meet. This aspect has a potential clash of interests now embedded in it.

Time schedules   The creation of time schedules, also, is an area full of difficulty if the persons involved have different cultural origins and, therefore, have different notions of how long things should take.

The term 'chronemics' has been applied to the timing of verbal exchange during conversations. British people normally expect people with whom they are having conversations to respond fairly quickly to their statements. In some other cultures, people time their exchanges to leave silences between each statement. For British people this can be unnerving and leads them to judge the other as shy or inattentive or bored. As a way of coping with this discomfort British people can end up repeating themselves, paraphrasing, talking louder and using other strategies to cope with the apparent silences of the other (silences incidentally that are absolutely appropriate and conventional from their own cultural domain).

Verbal behaviour

This is a much more obvious division between cultures, especially where languages differ. However, even in the case of both participants using the same language, the use of similar words may have different meanings or there will be different conventions for expressing opinion, etc. The capacity to which empathy may be extended to culturally different others may be quite limited.

Also not only what is said but how things are said (paralinguistics) have significantly different meanings for different cultures. Ums, ahs, sighs, grunts, accent, intonation, stress, pitch, are all culturally determined. Similarly, how the information is structured, who manages the conversation and who says what and when, falls within culturally determined conventions.

Non-verbal behaviour

Cultural differences in non-verbal behaviour can be categorized as follows:

Kinesics
These are movements of various parts of the body. Gestures in one country may well be quite inappropriate in another country.

Oculesics
This refers to the use or avoidance of eye-to-eye contact. The British use eye contact as a sign of listening behaviour. Research in the United States has demonstrated that many American black people listened with their ears and looked elsewhere, which proved disconcerting for white speakers who considered they had not been heard! The white Americans were not aware that they listened with their eyes as much as their ears. In many countries there are elaborate patterns of eye avoidance which are often linked to considerations of deferential respect for elders, those in authority and so on.

Haptics (touch)
Where, how and how often people touch each other while conversing are culturally determined patterns of behaviour.

The differences of role, class, and status are also arenas for considerable confusion between cultures because the various signals and cues to infer these positions are often quite invisible to outsiders.

Context

Hall draws broad definitions between what he terms high context and low context cultures. Examples of high context cultures are the Chinese, the Japanese and some Middle Eastern countries. Low context cultures tend to be in the west.

In low context cultures words are presumed to carry all meaning. In some cultures, words and meaning do not have such a direct connection. Notions of truth, consequently, are relative and culturally based. In low context cultures, there is also a tendency towards fragmentation of experience evidenced by the development of all sorts of experts and a proliferation of legalistic documents and contract.

By contrast, high context cultures tend towards conservative, rigid class structures where individual needs are sacrificed to group goals. However, these are cultures in which 'a person's word is their bond'. The context of a meeting carries the meaning, not simply the words used.

The work of Geert Hofstede

The following data represent the outcome of research carried out by Hofstede among employees of subsidiaries of one large US-based multinational corporation in 40 countries around the globe. 116,000 questionnaires were sent to a range of employees, from unskilled workers to top managers. Twenty languages were used in different versions of the questionnaire. This research (1967–73) was crossreferenced with other crosscultural research studies and statistically significant similarities were achieved.

We have already stated that Hofstede (1980) defines culture as the collective mental programming of a people in an environment. Culture is thus not a characteristic of individuals; it encompasses a number of people who were conditioned by the same education and life experience.

Hofstede (1980) argues strongly that because culture is characterized through collective mental programming, cultural change may only ever occur with difficulty and will take time. This is explained by the fact that it has become crystallized by the people within the wide variety of institutions and practices they have constructed together. These include educational, legal, governmental, religious, work, social and other organizational settings as well as their scientific theories.

For a set of 40 independent nations Hofstede tried to determine empirically the main criteria by which to judge how their national cultures differed. He found four such criteria, which he labelled dimensions; these were power distance, uncertainty avoidance, individualism collectivism, and masculinity femininity. They are described more fully below.

Figure 4.2   The power distance dimension

Small power distance	Large power distance
Inequality in society should be minimized.	There should be an order of inequality in this world in which everybody has a rightful place; high and low are protected by this order.
Hierarchy means an inequality of roles, established for convenience.	Hierarchy means existential inequality.
The use of power should be legitimate and is subject to the judgement as to whether it is good or evil.	Power is a basic fact of society that antedates good or evil. Its legitimacy is irrelevant.
All should have equal rights.	Power holders are entitled to privileges.
The way to change a social system is to redistribute power.	The way to change a social system is to dethrone those in power.
People at various power levels feel less threatened and more prepared to trust people.	Other people are a potential threat to one's power and can rarely be trusted.

Power distance

The first dimension of cultural difference Hofstede called power distance. It indicates the extent to which a society accepts the fact that power in institutions and organizations is distributed unequally. It is reflected in the values of the less powerful members of society as well as in those of the more powerful ones. A partial picture of these different value assumptions is shown in Figure 4.2. (There are many more examples in Hofstede 1980).

Uncertainty avoidance

The second dimension, uncertainty avoidance, indicates the extent to which a society feels threatened by uncertain and ambiguous situations and tries to avoid these situations by providing greater career stability, establishing more formal rules, not tolerating deviant ideas and behaviours, and believing in absolute truths and the attainment of expertise. Nevertheless, societies in which uncertainty avoidance is strong are also characterized by a higher level of anxiety and aggressiveness that creates, among other things, a stronger inner urge in people to work hard (see Figure 4.3).

Figure 4.3   The uncertainty avoidance dimension

Weak uncertainty avoidance	Strong uncertainty avoidance
The uncertainty inherent in life is more easily accepted and each day is taken as it comes.	The uncertainty inherent in life is felt as a continuous threat that must be fought.
Ease and lower stress are experienced.	Higher anxiety and stress are experienced.
Aggressive behaviour is frowned upon.	Aggressive behaviour of self and others is accepted.
Less showing of emotions is preferred.	More showing of emotions is preferred.
There is more willingness to take risks in life.	There is great concern with security in life.
The accent is on relativism, empiricism.	The search is for ultimate, absolute truths and values.
If rules cannot be kept, we should change them.	If rules cannot be kept, we are sinners and should repent.

Individualism collectivism

The third dimension encompasses individualism and its opposite, collectivism. Individualism implies a loosely knit social framework in which people are supposed to take care of themselves and their immediate families only, while collectivism is characterized by a tight social framework in which people distinguish between in-groups and out-groups; they expect their in-group (relatives, clan, organizations) to look after them, and in exchange for that they feel they owe absolute loyalty to it. A fuller picture of this dimension is presented in Figure 4.4.

Masculinity femininity

Measurements in terms of this dimension express the extent to which the dominant values in society are 'masculine', that is, whether they show assertiveness and approve of the acquisition of money and things; in contrast to 'feminine' values of caring for others and showing concern for the quality of life or people. The former values were labelled 'masculine' because, within nearly all societies, men scored higher in terms of the values' positive sense

Figure 4.4 The individualism collectivism dimension

Collectivist	Individualist
In society, people are born into extended families or clans who protect them in exchange for loyalty.	In society, everybody is supposed to take care of him/herself and his/her immediate family.
'We' consciousness holds sway.	'I' consciousness holds sway.
Identity is based in the social system.	Identity is based in the individual.
There is emotional dependence of individuals on organizations and institutions.	There is emotional independence of the individual from organizations
Belief is placed in group decisions.	Belief is placed in individual decisions.
Value standards differ for in-groups and out-groups (particularism).	Value standards should apply to all (universalism).

Figure 4.5 The masculinity femininity dimension

Feminine	Masculine
Men need not be assertive, but can also assume nurturing roles.	Men should be assertive. Women should be nurturing.
Sex roles in society are more fluid.	Sex roles in society are clearly differentiated.
Quality of life is important.	Performance is what counts.
You work in order to live.	You live in order to work.
People and environment are important.	Money and things are important.
Interdependence is the ideal.	Independence is the ideal.

(for example, they were more assertive than women), even though the society as a whole might veer towards the 'feminine' pole. Interestingly, the more an entire society scored to the masculine side, the wider the gap between its men's and women's values (see Figure 4.5).

An example is given in Figure 4.6 of one of the graphs developed by Hofstede, from his findings, charting the relative location of different cultures one to another along the dimensions of power distance and uncertainty avoidance.

Hofstede's work has been immensely influential in the field of international management but, as yet, it seems not to have filtered into this particular discipline. Counsellors who are actively engaged in transcultural work might

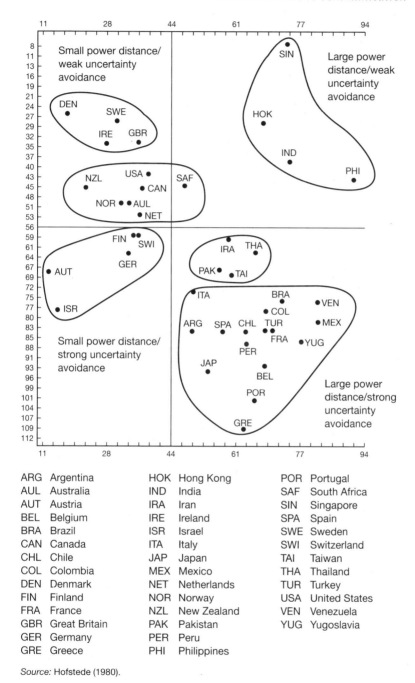

ARG   Argentina   HOK   Hong Kong   POR   Portugal
AUL   Australia   IND   India   SAF   South Africa
AUT   Austria   IRA   Iran   SIN   Singapore
BEL   Belgium   IRE   Ireland   SPA   Spain
BRA   Brazil   ISR   Israel   SWE   Sweden
CAN   Canada   ITA   Italy   SWI   Switzerland
CHL   Chile   JAP   Japan   TAI   Taiwan
COL   Colombia   MEX   Mexico   THA   Thailand
DEN   Denmark   NET   Netherlands   TUR   Turkey
FIN   Finland   NOR   Norway   USA   United States
FRA   France   NZL   New Zealand   VEN   Venezuela
GBR   Great Britain   PAK   Pakistan   YUG   Yugoslavia
GER   Germany   PER   Peru
GRE   Greece   PHI   Philippines

Source: Hofstede (1980).

Figure 4.6 The position of 40 countries on the power distance and uncertainty avoidance scales

be assisted immensely in their attempts at understanding specific clients through consulting Hofstede's original work. The graphic representation of culturally determined values that depict the relative positions between one culture and another, provide a unique and readily accessible mechanism for hypothesizing the potential value differences that lie between the counsellor and their client.

Nevertheless, this material, however useful, must also be used cautiously. Similar to the models of cultural and racial identity formation discussed elsewhere in this book, these ideas are generalized findings gleaned from wide research. They, therefore, cannot be attributed, unthinkingly, to every particular client, or indeed counsellor.

The above work, then, may be used most appropriately as a further background information source to assist the counsellor in their task. However these models must not be used as diagnostic or predictive tools. They can support an overall attempt at understanding but they cannot replace the moment to moment, attentive counselling relationship that is focused upon each client's specific and unique difficulties.

The iceberg conception of culture

Figure 4.7 has been used as a teaching aid in the field of international business relations. It is a particularly useful diagram in that it offers a list of interpersonal styles and expectations that pertain to the professional arena, and can consequently be modified and applied to the counselling task.

Summing up

> On the one hand we believe strongly that all forms of counselling are cross cultural, that cultural issues need to be seen as central to cross-cultural counselling (not ancillary) and that by focusing just on ethnic minority issues, we may be 'ghettoizing' the problem. Yet, we believe that multicultural counselling is a speciality area as well. Although all of us are racial, ethnic and cultural beings, belonging to a particular group does not endow a person with the competencies and skills necessary to be a culturally skilled counsellor.
>
> (Sue et al. 1992: 478)

This chapter has offered a very wide range of ideas concerning cultural differences in behaviour. This considerable range of information has deliberately been included to demonstrate the enormous extent of the potential behavioural differences that could occur between counsellors and their culturally different clients.

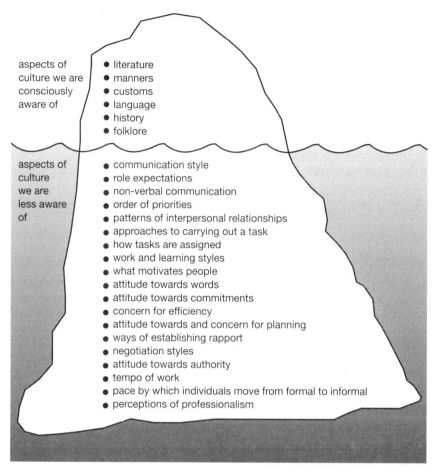

Figure 4.7   The iceberg conception of the nature of culture
Source: American Field Services (p. 14)

In Britain, for example, counsellors working with recently arrived nationals from other countries (refugees, international students, victims of torture, asylum seekers, international business persons, etc.) may find this information extremely useful and applicable.

Where counsellors are meeting clients who have lived in the dominant culture a significant proportion of their lives (or indeed all of them), yet have culturally different origins, then the subtleties of cultural identity and behaviour might become more obscure. Indeed, such clients may be biculturally competent and feel very comfortable operating out of both sets of cultural assumptions (those of the dominant culture and those of their own root culture). On the other hand, phenomena may occur in the interview that are confusing and misleading to both parties, and the counsellor might profitably gain from trying to understand these as cultural phenomena in action.

Counsellors must also be aware that cultural differences, however useful as a way of contributing understanding to interpersonal dialogue, can be used to conceal from the counsellor their own prejudiced and racist tendencies. Chapter 2, which discusses issues of race and power has to be held in balance with Chapters 3 and 4 in order to achieve a more balanced understanding of the overall dynamics in the counsellor/client relationship.

—5

Communication, language and gesture

Thinking follows a network of tracks laid down in the given language, an organisation which may concentrate systematically upon certain aspects of intelligence and may systematically discard others featured by other languages. The individual is utterly unaware of this organisation and is constrained completely within its unbreakable bonds.

(Whorf 1956: 256)

Promoting bilingualism rather than monolingualism should be a major goal to the provision of mental health services: it is an expression of personal freedom and pluralism.

(Sue et al. 1992: 479)

Introduction

All models of counselling/psychotherapy rely substantially on the process of talking and listening. Communication comprises both the form and the content of the counselling interview. The early sections of this chapter refer to the use of spoken language. Aspects of non-verbal communication are discussed later.

Whorf's statement above alerts us to a likely major predicament in the therapeutic process. Within the British situation, for example, there are likely to be (potentially) many combinations of counsellor and client having different linguistic origins. Some of these hypothesized combinations are:

1 Counsellor and client have totally different languages (e.g. English and Gujerati).
2 Counsellor and client use English in the interview though for one of them, English is their second language.
3 Both counsellor and client have apparently similar language origins but have grown up in different countries, e.g. an English counsellor with an American client.
4 Both counsellor and client have similar country and language origins but hail from different class positions from within that country.

The predicament that any combination of the above participants in counselling find themselves in is that of potentially misunderstanding the other. Language has no existence apart from the social reality of its users, argues Suzanne Romaine in her book *Language in Society* (1994). One wonders about the nature of that social reality of the client/counsellor relationship, if both parties speak different languages, as in example 1 above; or indeed, differences in fluency, accent and dialect, as depicted by examples 2, 3 and 4. All the scenarios suggest the creation of a social reality in the counsellor's room full of potential strain, exasperation and alienation. Being misunderstood begets anger, frustration, even hatred. By contrast, to be understood evokes trust, gratitude, exploration, love and aspiration. The use of language is absolutely central to the communication process and however much good intent there is, on both sides of a conversation, if misunderstandings persist then the potential for therapy is substantially diminished if not stopped altogether.

Language, thought and experience

As Whorf (1956) and Beattie (1964) remind us, people's categories of thought and the forms of their language are inextricably bound together. Whorf and Sapir were two of the earliest descriptive linguists to hint at the close relationship between language and thought (Mandelbaum 1940). According to Hall (1976a), Whorf's greatest contribution to western thinking lay in his meticulous description of the relationship of language to events in a crosscultural context. He demonstrated that cultures have unique ways of relating language to reality. This can be one of our principal sources of information concerning cultural differences. Nothing happens in the world of humans that is not deeply influenced by linguistic form.

If both language and thought are closely related, then so too is the connection between language and experience. Sapir has suggested that:

> The relation between language and experience is often misunderstood
> ... [it] actually defines experience for us by reason of its formal
> completeness and because of our unconscious projection of its implicit
> expectations into the field of experience. . . . Language is much like a
> mathematical system which ... becomes elaborated into a self-
> contained conceptual system which previsages all possible experience in
> accordance with certain accepted formal limitations . . . Categories such
> as number, gender, case, tense, mode, voice, 'aspect' and a host of others
> ... are not so much discovered in experience as imposed upon it . . .
>
> (Sapir 1931: 578)

Language, then, potentially limits experience. A problematic question is now posed as to whether a particular experience is available to someone who does not have the words to define it. Bram (1956) points out that a range of experience may be differentiated in the lexicon of one language and undifferentiated in another. Thus, taking the perception of colours in different cultures, Leff (1973) reports that Pacific Island languages do not distinguish between blue and green and the Navaho only have one word for grey and brown. Bram's point is that though the full range of colour-perceiving apparatus is present in Pacific Islanders and Navaho Indians, linguistically and practically they do not make as much use of its differentiating ability as some other peoples. By contrast, a classic example of high differentiation in linguistic category and practical usage is the considerable range of words for types of snow possessed by Laplanders.

Language, emotion and meaning

The links between language, experience, emotion and meaning can become rather more tenuous in abstract subjects. For example, if another person states 'I see a car', and there is a car in our shared visual field, then both of us assume we are sharing a common perceptual experience. However, where there is no external, concrete referent, as in the statement 'I feel sad', the assumption of a common experience rests on more delicate grounds. Counselling and psychotherapy rely on the process of communication. Much of the substance of counselling is often communication about communicating (e.g. the counsellor is told about the client's communication with other people). Further, the client's emotional state is often mentioned and focused upon. Thus statements such as the one quoted above, 'I feel sad', is potentially hazardous to the whole process of mutual understanding, especially in transcultural settings.

This implementation of the concept of empathy often demands that the counsellor attempt to 'imagine' what the client is experiencing in his or her situation, perhaps through a comparison of a 'similar' experience of their own. Quite clearly, in a crosscultural situation, this urge towards understanding enters the realm of possibly inadequate approximations, or at worst, hit-or-miss hypotheses. As indicated above, there are no reliable external referents. In addition, for emotions, there are no scientific measures available to help us. Leff (1973) examined the attempts that have been made to differentiate the measurement of physiological arousal in various emotional states. Emotional states can be measured via physiological manifestations, but these measurements could not differentiate between the differing emotional states – specifically different emotional states manifest similar physical symptoms.

Hall (1976a) has used a notion called 'extension transference' which, when applied to language and experience, becomes a useful theoretical concept. Thus, spoken language is a symbolization of something that happened, is happening or will happen. Written language as an extension of the spoken form is therefore a symbolization of symbolization! The extension can become confused with or takes the place of the process described.

This process of extension transference would seem to fit with Leff's (1973) hypotheses of a scheme for the historical development of words denoting emotional states. Where previously one word may have existed to denote a pattern of physiological response, it is likely that that word came to denote an emotional state or experience as well as the somatic condition. The focus of meaning subsequently shifted to the experiencing of emotion and the somatic meaning faded into the background. Thus an extension transference has taken place. Finally, in the historic development of the word, it is likely that it split up into phonetically related variants, as the global state was differentiated into several smaller categories.

The possibility of accurate translation and conveyance of meaning appears to become even less possible! Maw (1980) has reported initial difficulties in responding to African students within a British student health service, where presenting complaints had been of itching sensations in the head or of stomach-ache. Despite closer physical inspection and treatment, the symptoms persisted. Consultations with African medical colleagues, however, revealed the possibility that the students were suffering anxiety or depression. The direct translation of their language into English revealed its use of the somatic interpretations of the experience rather than the emotional one.

Other research comparing use of language across classes (lower, middle, upper) and groups of different economic levels has revealed similar tendencies to express emotional distress in quite different ways, from the concrete somatic to much more abstract and abstruse descriptions (Crandel and Dohrenwend 1967; Bernstein 1971).

'I love her', 'I have a pain in my gut', 'My soul is injured by this' are all statements that have a myriad of meanings. Assumptions of readily understanding every client statement are fraught with danger for counsellors and psychotherapists.

There is a temptation, also, to disparage others' language forms as deficient. As with the concept of culture, others' language forms are different, not deficient. Pinker's (1994) study of humanity's capacity for language points to the variety of mechanisms all languages and dialects employ. The counsellor needs to appreciate and respect fully the sophistication of all communication forms used by clients.

The process of the development of any language inevitably involves the selective development of a specific number of sounds for the purposes of that spoken language or dialect. Differentiation thus occurs in this selection, for as Benedict (1968) points out, the number of sounds that can be produced by our vocal cords and our oral and nasal cavities is practically unlimited. Power wrote (1981) that, in linguistic terms, there seems to be no reason why people should not learn new languages and be able to speak them without a trace of accent from their first language. However, one of the hurdles to this development is the previous exposure to the selection of sounds available in the first language, which serves to blunt the listening sensitivity to a new combination of sounds.

The process of differentiation is one determined by cultural demands:

> Each individual creates the systems for his verbal behaviour so that they shall resemble those of the group or groups with which, from time to time, he may wish to be identified, to the extent that:
> (a) He can identify the groups
> (b) He has both opportunity and ability
> (c) His motivation is sufficiently strong to impel him to choose and to adapt his behaviour accordingly and
> (d) He is still able to adapt his behaviour.
>
> (Le Page 1968)

A rather simplistic extension of this idea is the example of therapists who inappropriately attempt to use slang that they believe is representative of the client's dialect as a way of establishing rapport with the client. This, of course, can often be viewed as condescending (Hunt 1987) and will certainly work against the success of the counselling process.

The limits of language

The relationship between language, thought and experience is one of great complexity, with the implication being that both thought and experience are dominated and limited by language. When learning about another culture the limitations of language are shown up. Hall (1976a) describes language as: 'by nature poorly adapted to this difficult task ... it is too linear, not comprehensive enough, too slow, too limited, too constrained, too un-natural, too much a product of its own evolution . . .'

Becker (1972) reports Harry Stack Sullivan's hypothesis that words are basic to the formation of a child's self concept and are the only way by which that child can control his or her environment. Becker takes this hypothesis and develops it considerably in his suggestion that what we term 'personality' is largely a locus of word possibilities: 'When we expose our self-esteem to possible undermining by others in a social situation, we are exposing a linguistic identity to other loci of linguistic causality' (p. 99).

In support of this somewhat mechanistic and most certainly reductionist notion of language, he also quotes Dale Carnegie: 'It matters not what you mean: you and those around you become according to what you say' (p. 100).

Thus, extracting the essence from the above range of views, language not only restricts thought and experience but also tends to limit others' perceptions of you to your language. The implications of such a reductionist view of language are really considerable and somewhat pessimistic. The enormous attention paid to this subject by many of Britain's philosophers and sociologists in the earlier decades of this century has tended not only to 'abolish the "subject", but turn language into an autonomous and dominating entity' (Sharrock et al. 1981)

It is our view, however, that transcultural issues must not be reduced to the limiting interpretations of the function of language and language differences.

Despite the fact that both Whorf and Sapir were considerably ahead of their time in their hypotheses, Hall (1976a) notes that they fall into the 'extension transference' trap, i.e. they believed that language was thought. This counterassertion is most important to the subject under consideration. Language clearly is not thought.

> As for the idea that language limits thought . . . there are some meaty problems posed by Chomsky's arguments. If language is an infinitely productive resource, how are we to determine what cannot be said or thought in it, how are we to survey the possibilities available to it?
>
> (Sharrock et al. 1981)

Considered from this perspective, language has potential for infinite creativity and is subject to the speaker's capacity for ingenuity, invention and figurative, idiomatic and allusive expression. Taken from this philosophic stance, language always has the potential to express thought and to acknowledge experience. As counselling philosophy implicitly recognizes the potential for growth in people, it would seem important to consider that the nature of language within the counselling process always has the potential of achieving its task of articulating the clients' agenda. In addition, a reciprocal task lies in the counsellor's domain, that of developing this sensitivity to, knowledge of and skill in their client's communication forms.

Language and power

> '. . . the proper word or phrase, properly delivered, is the highest attainment of human interpersonal power'
>
> (Becker 1972: 100).

Both Sarup (1978) and Freire (1972) have recognized the need for minority groups (political, ethnic, economic) to be helped towards recognizing and possessing their 'word', the *logos*. For once recognized, the 'word' cannot be minimized or deleted and, at best, should enable people to achieve greater self-confidence, more effective communication and greater understanding of their predicament.

The process of counselling, with its accent on acceptance, listening and dialogue, has the potential to provide persons from minority groups or low-esteem positions with the opportunity to speak, practice, experiment with and thus create and develop their 'word', their symbols of meaning. Counselling, in this sense, has a very political outcome. It can help equip clients with a language and a confidence derived from their own explorations of their situation.

A counter to this radical and hopeful view is provided by Romaine (1994), who argues that questions of language are also questions of power. Certain ways of speaking are perceived as superior largely because they are used by the powerful. If the counsellor is (or perceived to be) part of a powerful elite in society (for example, in the UK the majority of counsellors/psychotherapists are white, middle class, and often very articulate), then their very way of speaking and being may be perceived as so superior that the client is driven further into silence and self-doubt. The effect of the client's perception of and projections on to the counsellor can be so determining here that little successful work may ensue between them.

This phenomenon also demands that the counsellor becomes fully aware of the potential impact of their accent, dialect and vocabulary upon others.

Of particular concern here is the counsellor's own understanding of their political position in relation to the issues of racism and their own discourse. The scholarly work of Van Dijk points to those groups

> who define the moderate mainstream . . . all those who thus manage public opinion, dominant ideologies and consensual everyday practices. It is our claim that white group dominance in general, and racism in particular, . . . pre-suppose a creative process in which these moderate elites play a crucial role. . . . For most members of elite groups, this thesis is hard to swallow, being fundamentally inconsistent with their normative self-concept. After all, elites often see themselves as moral leaders and will therefore generally dissociate themselves from anything that has to do with racism as they define it. As a consequence . . . conclusions of research on racism and accusations of minority groups are often denied, marginalised, or even violently attacked by elites, who thereby, precisely confirm the plausibility of the thesis.
>
> (Van Dijk 1993: 9)

Many counsellors will, as a matter of course, deny their part as being members of elite groups; quite obviously they are not politicians, journalists or media persons who shape views and attitudes through language. However, they are, in many cases, related to the elite groups in society by virtue of their class, their education, their profession and so on.

Counsellor discourse, with their clients and with their colleagues and friends, has to be examined by itself in order to understand further the implications of its effect upon minority group clients. Van Dijk notes (p. 80) that the statement 'we are reasonable and rational' is of course a standard ideological proposition of Eurocentrism. Denials of racism are also the stock-in-trade of racist discourse (p. 81).

This section demonstrates the complex relationship between language and power. If the client, through psychotherapy, develops their language, a confidence in their view of the world, much has been achieved. On the other hand, the therapist must pay attention to their use of language and its potential negative effects upon clients.

Linguistic differences and translation

> Culturally skilled counsellors take responsibility for interacting in the language requested by the client: this may mean appropriate referral to outside sources. A serious problem arises when the linguistic skills of the counsellor do not match the language of the client. This being the case, counsellors should (a) seek a translator with cultural knowledge and appropriate professional background or (b) refer to a knowledgeable and competent bilingual counsellor.
>
> (Sue et al. 1992: 438)

The quote, above, is taken from a key article in the development of multicultural counselling in the United States. The article proposes 31 multicultural counselling competencies which, it is hoped, the American counselling profession will adopt as part of their accreditation criteria. A more extended exposition may be found in Chapter 11.

The above proposition by Sue et al. certainly throws down the challenge to many counselling practitioners in the UK today. Britons are well known (perhaps a little stereotypically) as being generally unskilled and a little reluctant in the learning and acquisition of other languages. A certain cultural over-reliance seems to exist on the fact that English is one of the most widely spoken international languages. Therefore the attitude seems to be 'why bother?'. This simplistic sketch does not do full justice, of course, to thousands of schoolchildren, college and university students studying other languages formally or to many adults who pursue language courses in their leisure time. Nevertheless, within the counselling profession the authors know of few cases where counsellors have set out to develop their knowledge of specific languages because of the client groups they are working with. It has always been easier to assume that clients will need to converse in English.

The proposition contains the phrase that 'counsellors take responsibility for interacting in the language requested by the client'. There will be many circumstances in which the client, for a variety of reasons, would not make such a request.

For that reason we suggest moving towards a recommendation that incorporates the following sentiments. 'Culturally skilled counsellors take the responsibility for ensuring that the client's preference for language within the counselling interview is respected.' This implies that counsellors would have to seek the views and wishes of clients as to the language used in the interviews. If, in doing so, they found out that a language other than English was required, it is likely that a crisis would ensue, the crisis being how to continue.

The proposition incorporates the possibilities of using either a translator or referral to another bilingual counsellor. The translator should be someone 'with cultural knowledge and appropriate professional background'. These criteria are both relatively specific yet may be interpreted with some elasticity and discretion. Clearly there are many advantages in the use of translators. These include:

- Their use infers respect for the client's preferred language.
- They signal to the client the counsellor's wish to understand fully the client and their predicament.
- They acknowledge that the client will be able to be maximally fluent and descriptive of their situation in their own language.

However, the use of translators is not without difficulty and counsellors need to be fully aware of the limitations translation might impose. The use of translators immediately reduces the possibility of direct communication (see Figure 5.1) between client and counsellor, and substitutes a more indirect model (Figure 5.2). The counsellor may hope for and assume that the translator provides a clear technical function (see Figure 5.3). (It is recognized that direct communication was already probably not possible.)

However, the persona of the translator has to be taken into account. Thus, the communication process becomes even more complex (see Figure 5.4). Messages relayed from the counsellor and client have to pass through the technical and the personal aspects of the translator. The translator, as a human being, is subject to the same difficulties that a counsellor is in terms of attitudes, assumptions, cultural origins and so on. The counsellor may make statements which the translator considers cannot be interpreted directly, for example, such statements may be culturally insensitive or impolite or the translator may be so embarrassed themselves by the question that they change the meaning of it or they may consider that to give the counsellor certain cultural information would be to let the culture down in the face of outsiders.

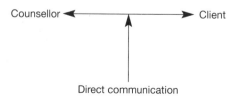

Figure 5.1 Direct communication between counsellor and client

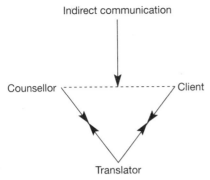

Figure 5.2   Indirect communication between counsellor and client through a translator

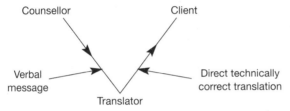

Figure 5.3   Direct, technically correct translation of counsellor message to client

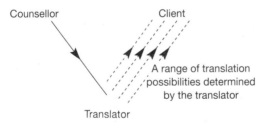

Figure 5.4   Indirect personalized translation of counsellor message to client

In short, the messages that leave both the counsellor and client have the potential to be modified and indeed changed through the translator.

The impact of the move from two persons to three in the counselling interaction has to be accommodated by the counsellor's skill and capacity to work with the increased dynamics as shown in the differences between Figures 5.5 and 5.6.

The counsellor will have to establish a credible working alliance with the

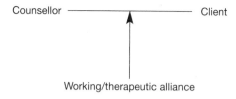

Figure 5.5   Therapeutic alliance between counsellor and client

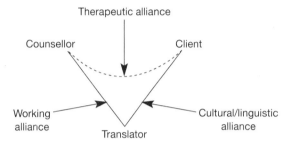

Figure 5.6   Different alliances between counsellor, translator and client

translator for and on behalf of the potential success of the counselling process. The therapeutic alliance is therefore 'bent' through the translator. At the same time a natural cultural alliance may form between the client and the translator. Both this and the earlier scenario demonstrates how the translator quickly moves from being a technical addition to the interview to enhance its effectiveness to being a significantly more complex component in the process.

The extent to which each of the participants in this three-way relationship are able fully to trust the other two persons may determine the capacity to which the client is helped. Figure 5.7 may make this structure clearer.

To what extent can the client dare to reveal or be more of their 'real selves', to trust the counsellor and translator more? To what extent can the translator understand the work of the counsellor and become an ally to the therapeutic process? To what extent can the counsellor skilfully incorporate all these additional facets within the counselling encounter without becoming sabotaged by the demands of this situation?

The above points serve to illustrate how working with a translator can complicate the counselling process. This fact does not deny, however, the underlying importance of having translation available in certain circumstances. Counsellors will need, though, to consider much more systematically how to manage such three-way situations in order that they can fully involve translators and prepare clients for the impact of this new working situation.

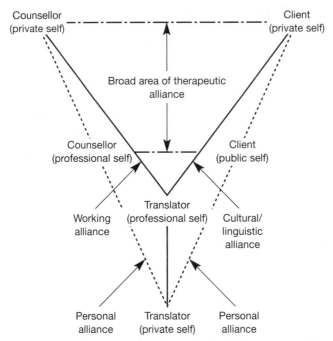

Figure 5.7   The personal and professional dimensions of the various working alliances

Paralinguistics

> The learning of another's language is not enough ... unless you understand the subtle cues implicit in language, tone, gesture and expression ... you will not only consistently misinterpret what is said to you, but you may offend irretrievably without knowing how or why'.
>
> (Hall 1976b: 66–74)

Paralinguistics is the name given to the manner in which language is voiced. It comprises aspects of language which include accent, tone, volume, pitch, sighs, ums, ahs, grunts and silences.

Gumperz et al. (1981) also use the term 'prosody', which incorporates intonation, pitch and rhythm, pronoun preferences and the way information is structured in discourse. Clearly, all these have an effect on the interpretation of meaning and intent.

Confirming the quote by Hall above, Gumperz and his colleagues acknowledge the subconscious control of these features in speech. Additionally, speakers cannot use, interpret or often even recognize any alternative system to their own. 'Prosodic' conventions, therefore, when not shared (e.g.

in a counselling encounter where both persons have different linguistic origins), can cause considerable misunderstandings.

The systematic and long-term research by Gumperz et al. has been most important in identifying various processes of paralinguistic convention that serve to irritate and miscommunicate between persons of differing cultural backgrounds. A BBC TV programme made in the early 1980s provided a demonstration of a particular form of indirect racial discrimination which can occur as a result of 'prosodic' features in speech. Various scenes are depicted in the programme in which the ebb and flow of interpersonal communication between two people of differing cultural backgrounds is monitored. Each conversation that is shown (a transaction in a bank, a social security interview and a job interview) demonstrates the adverse effects of culturally different patterns of intonation in sentences and how speeches are structured.

As a result of implicit judgements, irritations and miscommunications felt and made by the interviewer (most often, in the UK, a person from the majority white culture) the culturally different client is likely to suffer indirect discrimination as a consequence of being misunderstood.

Recent research in sociolinguistics shows that a major contributory factor in this type of indirect discrimination can be the result of subconscious processes of evaluation during conversation on the part of majority and minority users of English. In this process, both parties tend to judge the other's behaviour in terms of criteria which they do not share and do not verbalize. These criteria have to do with the way we assess the quality and adequacy of what is said (Gumperz et al. 1981).

These findings reveal that the learning of another's language is often not enough to communicate successfully. One also needs to understand the subtle cues implicit in language, tone, gestures and expression, if consistent misinterpretation and irretrievable offence is to be avoided.

A simple example of the adverse effects of paralinguistics is quoted in Hall (1976a) concerning the loudness with which one speaks. In Saudi Arabian cultures, in discussions among equals, the men attain a decibel level that would be considered aggressive, objectionable and obnoxious in the United States. Loudness connotes strength and sincerity among Arabs; a soft tone implies weakness and deviousness. Personal status also modulates voice tone. Lower classes lower their voices. Thus, if a Saudi Arab shows respect to an American he lowers his voice. Americans 'ask' people to talk louder by actually speaking louder. The Arab then has his status confirmed and thus talks even quieter. Both are misreading the cues!

Non-verbal communication

'For in the final analysis every important cultural gesture comes down to a morality, a model for human behaviour concentrated into a gesture' (Hesse

1979: 44). Non-verbal behaviour, as a communication system, can often cause miscommunication across cultures.

Aspects of non-verbal behaviour have already been covered in Chapter 4, namely, the uses of space and the concepts of time. Other significant areas still require articulation. Among these are included: patterns of eye contact, styles of dress, bodily signals, emotional displays, greetings behaviours, other forms of self-presentation (e.g. gift giving and visiting-cards), rituals and facial expressions.

Argyle (1975) focused some attention on the problematic dichotomy between the biological and cultural origins of non-verbal communication. He asserts that there is good evidence that some bodily signals are biological. These signals apply to the main facial expressions and to laughing and crying (p. 74). He also quotes Eibl-Eibesfeldt (1972) who has found similar evidence of the universality of the 'eyebrow flash', in which eyebrows are raised to a maximum extent for about one sixth of a second, in greeting and flirting. However, there is some cultural variation even in these bodily signals. One dimension in which cultures vary, therefore, is in the extent to which facial expressions are restrained or shown freely.

Gestural signals present a rather different picture and often reflect and emphasize the cultural component of communication. Thus La Barre (1964) has listed the different hand movements with special meanings used in different cultures; a gesture from one culture would be meaningless in most other cultures. An important component to notice here is that though various cultures practice similar bodily movements, the meanings of such movements are very different to each culture.

Vaughan (1977) has cited several examples of non-verbal communication from a British viewpoint:

> In Ghana, our thumbs-up sign meaning O.K., that's alright, fine, great etc. is a grave insult which will attract severely disapproving glances, perhaps even a spell in prison. Our nod of the head for 'yes' and shake for 'no' have exactly the opposite meaning in Japan. To accept something with one hand, especially the left is greatly disrespectful in many, if not all African countries where children are taught very early to give and accept with both hands. Also in some countries you only eat with your right hand as the left hand is used for toilet purposes. Our ways of attracting attention may also appear rude to someone who uses their hands differently.

'Syncing'

Hall (1976a) cites studies of the use of movements in conversations between people. He uses the term 'syncing' from the observation that when two people talk to each other their movements often become synchronized. Hall suggests that in viewing films in slow motion, looking for synchrony, one realizes that what we know as dance is really a slowed-down stylized version of what human beings do whenever they interact.

These studies suggest that 'syncing' is panhuman. From this it appears that syncing is perhaps the most basic element of communication and the foundation upon which all subsequent speech behaviour rests.

Other aspects of this research revealed that very young English children 'synced' with Chinese children just as well as they did with English. As people grow older however, there are indications that people 'sync' within and are tied to each other by hierarchies of rhythms that are culture-specific and expressed through language and body movement. Thus kinesics (body movements) are culturally determined and must be viewed against a cultural backdrop.

Hall suggests that 'syncing' as a process of natural rhythm or 'dance' can affect people in their everyday situations; thus, for workers, when the talk slows, the work slows; also it is well known that sea shanties and work songs established rhythms of work.

Hall also analysed slow-motion films of children in school playgrounds and noticed both that 'pan-playground syncing' can occur (despite a lot of children playing various games) and that when syncing was absent or disturbed, socially disastrous effects were the result.

Given the possibility of 'syncing' in such a macro-situation Hall provides us with another theoretical understanding of the occurrence of 'atmosphere' in concerts and dances that are a success. He recognizes that music and dance operate as an extension transference of syncing. If audience and artist are syncing successfully, they are part of the same process, a socially rewarding experience.

Though interesting, the notion of 'syncing' may appear of only peripheral interest to us. However, within a counselling situation, it clearly has enormous implications for the quality of communication that occurs. The counsellor's task in a transcultural situation may be somewhat more difficult, however, owing to the culturally limited patterns that dictate the synchronous rhythms. Nevertheless, the degree to which a sense of synchronization is achieved in the ebb and flow of a counselling interview between client and counsellor may be an important indicator as to the effectiveness of what is happening therapeutically.

6

Western theories of counselling and psychotherapy: intentions and limitations

> My patients and their problems are not entirely separable from the outside
> environment they have created and in which they function. With a good
> conscience, I, as the psychotherapist, cannot divorce my patients from their
> social and cultural background; they are, after all, a specific group of
> people who have reacted in a specific way to their problems . . . a human
> being does not live in a sterilized plastic bubble.
>
> (Cooper 1984: 314)

Introduction

Therapists are profoundly and inevitably influenced in their counselling
practice by therapeutic theory. The theories by which they operate are often
acquired through the therapist's original training programme and then
reinforced or modified by their working environments. Thus, counsellors are
significantly influenced in the ways they approach, reflect upon and predict
the outcome of their work by the tutorial and theoretical influences they were
exposed to whilst in training or in post. These influences may be described in
terms of cultural imposition and acquisition. That is, the theories have been
handed down by senior representatives of the culture (counselling lecturers)
to the trainees or initiates who are then schooled in, and assessed according to
their successful acquisition of such principles.

Many of the current theories of therapy are rooted, historically, in central
European and more latterly North American culture. As such, these theories
are culturally and historically bound and as a consequence also have
limitations as to their applicability to all situations and persons in a
multicultural/multiracial society.

The range of therapeutic theories have been numbered as 481 distinct
models (Karasu et al. 1984) though it is widely recognized that there are three
or four broad categories or approaches into which the large number cited

above can be fitted. Often described as the first, second and third forces in psychology/counselling, they represent psychoanalytic, behavioural and humanistic ways of viewing human beings and their problems (Mahrer 1989).

A fourth force was historically ascribed to theories involving transpersonal/metaphysical dimensions though, interestingly, in very recent times in the United States, multiculturalism is becoming hailed by the same name, the fourth force (Pedersen 1991). This theme is revisited in later chapters.

Though there are clearly limitations as to the unthinking applicability of these theories we do know that counselling approaches are generally seen as valid, relevant and effective in western culture at this time (McLeod 1993). Indeed Wood (1990) has elaborated further on this theme of 'fit' between therapy and culture, recognizing the importance of cultural acceptability of the healing form. Describing counselling as a 'subtle but powerful ritual', he recognizes that the ritual may be on the cutting edge of cultural change. The relationship, therefore, between a culture and its healing rituals is an interesting and complex one. Society permits certain degrees of experimentation, indeed some rituals may run counter to other important cultural values. None the less the commanding principles of the ritual, the counselling process, are probably developed in response to emerging needs of the culture and probably lose effectiveness over time. One example of this loss of effectiveness could well be part of the original *raison d'être* of this book and others on the same theme. That is, the current forms and modes of counselling and psychotherapy are not proving to be adequate in response to the changing and contemporary needs of society.

The historic and cultural origins of counselling and psychotherapy

The historic and cultural origins of counselling are well presented by McLeod (1993: 8–16). Citing a range of sources, he asserts that the origins of counselling and psychotherapy as we know them today can be traced back to the beginning of the eighteenth century, which represents a turning point in the social construction of 'madness'. A shift occurred at this time, from dealing with problems encountered in living through religious perspectives implemented at community level towards the medicalization and individualization of human difficulties.

This historic period incorporates the major changes involved in society moving from a predominantly rural/agricultural base to an industrial one. Through the industrial revolution, capitalism began to dominate economic and political life and the values of science began to replace those of religion. In addition, Albee (1977) has argued that this emerging capitalism required the development of a high level of rationality accompanied by repression and control of pleasure seeking. This required the development of a work ethic, an increase in personal autonomy and independence. The accompanying psychological shift that occurred was from a 'tradition-centred' society to one in which inner direction was emphasized. A basis for this shift to secular individualism had already been laid by the philosopher, Descartes, in the seventeenth century (Flew 1972). Through recognizing the movement from small rural communities where everyone knew everyone else and behaviour was monitored and controlled by others, to urban industrial societies where life was much more anonymous and internally focused, one may understand some of the underlying historic conditions that have led to contemporary forms of interpersonal help, which focus on the individual, inner life of the person.

Prior to the eighteenth century, people who suffered mental ill health would have been nursed by their extended families and local communities. The advent of larger urban areas, factory conditions, fragmentation of communities and greater anonymity between people eventually led to the establishment of workhouses and asylums – society-based responses. People who were deemed mad or insane were certainly not productive and in many cases were disruptive. It is not appropriate here to provide a wealth of detail of this period, interesting though it is, but it is crucial to understand that through this historical period the medical profession came to assume control over asylums (Scull 1975). The defeat of moral treatment can be seen as a key moment in the history of psychotherapy: science replaced religion as the dominant ideology underlying the treatment of the insane (McLeod 1993).

New medical-biological explanations for insanity were formulated and many different types of physical treatment were experimented with (Scull 1979). By the end of the nineteenth century, psychiatry had achieved a dominant position in the care of the insane. According to Ellenberger (1970) the earliest physicians to call themselves psychotherapists were Van Renterghem and Van Eeden who opened a clinic of Suggestive psychotherapy in Amsterdam in 1887.

Altered states of consciousness and hypnosis

Through applying the theoretical constructs of ritual to the counselling process, Wood (1990) notes that the healing process provides the means for the client to enter an altered state of consciousness and offers a structure within which their personal experience may be constructively reorganized. There are a considerable number of references to altered states of consciousness in the next chapter, which deals with indigenous forms of healing; McLeod (1993) also cites several sources that have observed this important use of trance states and altered states of consciousness in the healing rituals of traditional societies. Indeed he asserts that the appearance of Mesmerism and hypnosis through the eighteenth and nineteenth centuries in Europe and their transformation into psychotherapy can be viewed as representing the assimilation of a traditional cultural form into modern scientific medicine. Instrumental in this process were the extraordinary contributions of the work of Sigmund Freud.

Sigmund Freud and psychoanalysis

> Such is the influence of Freud's work on European and American thought and culture, even in the popular mind, that it is difficult to imagine that time when his ideas were so innovative and, indeed, shocking.
>
> (Jacobs 1984: 23)

Sigmund Freud (1856–1939) was born to Jewish parents in Freiberg, Czechoslovakia, where he was one of a family of two boys and five girls. He apparently excelled at school, and though his interests were 'directed more towards human concerns than natural objects', medicine itself, though he chose to pursue it as a career, had not been a simple choice.

He trained initially as a neurologist, conducting research into the histology of nerve cells as part of his medical training (Nelson-Jones 1988). As a physician in the General Hospital of Vienna, he gained experience in several departments and became an active researcher in the Institute of Cerebral Anatomy, during which time he began to study nervous diseases. On the award of a travelling scholarship Freud went to Paris in 1885 to study under Charcot, whose research work was concerned with hysteria and who employed hypnotherapy as a major helping mechanism.

McLeod (1993: 12) points out that whilst not 'denying the genius and creativity of Freud, it is valuable to reflect on some of the ways in which his approach reflected the intellectual fashions and social practices of his time.' For example:

- Individual sessions with an analyst were an extension of normal practice of one-to-one doctor–patient consultations prevalent at that time.
- Freud's idea of a unitary life-force (libido) was derived from nineteenth-century biological theories.
- The idea that emotional problems had a sexual cause was widely accepted in the nineteenth century.
- The idea of the unconscious had already been employed not only by the hypnotists but also by other nineteenth-century writers and philosophers (p. 12).

'Freud's distinctive contribution', McLeod continues, 'can probably be regarded as his capacity to assimilate all of these ideas into a coherent theoretical model which has proved of great value in many fields of work' (p. 12). Indeed he has been described as 'striding like a colossus over the twentieth century'. His work has influenced many fields including psychology, philosophy, literature, literary and art criticism, psychiatry and social work practice. Words and phrases such as 'Freudian slip', the death instinct, the pleasure principle, defence mechanism and many more derive from his original works.

Freud developed his theoretical and clinical work in two major areas: the art, technique and practice of psychotherapy; and the theoretical development of ideas and concepts on the formation and nature of personality.

Nelson-Jones (1988) lists some of the major concepts and ideas developed by Freud. These include: the pleasure principle, the instincts, the unconscious and consciousness, the structure of mental apparatus (id, ego, superego), anxiety, psychical energy and bisexuality. In relation to the development of personality he wrote about infantile sexuality and amnesia, sexual development, identification, defence mechanisms (repression, sublimation, reaction-formation, denial, fixation, regression projection) and the development and perpetuation of neuroses. In developing psychoanalysis he used different techniques including hypnosis, free association, resistance, interpretation and the interpretation of dreams; he wrote extensively on the therapeutic relationship between patient and therapist (technically named as transference and countertransference).

Jacobs (1984) reminds us that Freudian theory arose from psychotherapy and not from formal research, quoting Winnicott, as a rider: 'It is more difficult for an analyst to be truly original than for anyone else, because everything we say, truly has been taught us yesterday, i.e. by patients!' (p. 26).

The extraordinary range of hypotheses developed by Freud and listed above dramatically extended the understanding of psychological complexity into the 'darker recesses of the soul'. During the same period new scientific discoveries which radically changed our view of the world were also being made. These included radioactivity, the nuclear atom, quantum theory, the rediscovery of Mendel's law of inheritance and the science of genetics. There is no doubt that Freud was therefore in the vanguard of scientific development, contributing to the major paradigm shifts that occurred in scientific development in the early decades of this century (Clark 1980).

One of the key developments in the move from psychoanalysis, which by and large was only accessible to the middle and upper classes, to counselling and psychotherapy as we know it today was the emigration of psychoanalysis to the United States (McLeod 1993).

> The rise of fascism in Europe led to several prominent analysts . . . moving to New York and Boston where they found a willing clientele. Compared to Europe, American society demonstrated a much greater degree of social mobility, with people being very likely to live, work and marry outside their original neighbourhood, town, social class or ethnic group. There were therefore many individuals who had problems in forming satisfactory relationships or having a secure sense of personal

identity. Moreover the 'American Dream' insisted that everyone could better themselves and emphasized the pursuit of happiness of the individual as a legitimate aim in life. Psychotherapy offered a fundamental, radical method of self-improvement.

(McLeod 1993: 13)

Behaviourism and the development of cognitive-behavioural therapy

American academic psychologists had become very interested in and influenced by behaviourism at the end of the First World War and were consequently somewhat resistant to this invasion of psychoanalytic thought and practice (as indeed they were to the development of the humanistic theories featured in the next section).

Based upon the work of the Russian psychologist, Pavlov (1849–1936) who developed theories of behaviour through conditioning in his animal research using dogs, theorists such as John Watson and Frederick Skinner applied their attention to human psychology.

Nelson-Jones (1988: 108) suggests that

as an overall theory the distinctive emphasis is on the overwhelming role of environmental contingencies in influencing the acquisition and perpetuation of behaviour. In its most radical form the behavioural model sees human actions as derived solely from two sources: biological deprivations, such as hunger and sexual tension and the individual's learning history.

In contrast to other forms of psychological treatment which emerged largely from clinical practice, behaviour therapy was regarded by its founders as the applied branch of a basic science. Since it had proved possible to create phobias experimentally through classical conditioning (Watson and Rayner 1920), it was argued that all neurotic disorders could be seen as inappropriate learned responses which could be 'unlearned' through the application of procedures devised from the work of Pavlov and Skinner. Thus Wolpe (1958) defined this approach as the use of experimentally established principles of learning for the purpose of changing unadaptive behaviour (Mackay 1984).

According to the original tenets of behaviourism, only actions that are observable and measurable can be studied scientifically. Hence only client problems which are specific and externally observable can be treated. Broadly speaking, behaviour therapists have denied the importance or verifiability of intrapsychic processes (Feltham and Dryden 1993). A variety of treatment techniques have been developed including systematic desensitization, implosion and operant conditioning; it has been noticed that behaviour therapy appears to be more successful in treating conditions such as obsessive-compulsive disorders, phobias and panic attacks.

Later work in the United States by Bandura (1969) and Kanfer and Phillips (1970) led to the development of cognitive change methods being used in conjunction with standard behavioural techniques. Feltham and Dryden (1993: 31) define cognitive-behavioural therapy as

> an umbrella term for those approaches based as, related to or developing from Behaviour therapy and Cognitive therapy . . . the core concept of cognitive-behavioural therapy is that beliefs about events in our lives are open to examination and change, and that changing beliefs results in greater control of our lives and reduction in dysfunctional behaviour. A hallmark of all these approaches is their clinical insistence on changing behaviour through the interrelationship of cognition and behaviour.

The technology of early forms of behaviour therapy has now given way to the development of effective coping strategies. 'Technology has been replaced, to a large extent, by talking treatments' (Mackay 1984: 266).

The cognitive-behavioural construct depicts human beings as people concerned to see themselves as being in control of their environment, both in their internal and external worlds. They are happiest when they have evolved a clear plan for living, when their body behaves as they want it to and when they have the skills and aptitudes necessary to achieve the goals they set themselves (Mackay 1984). This 'success and control-focused' model is certainly consistent with a view of western individuals held by Palmer (1991) who also extends this concept to a western belief that nature itself exists to serve individuals.

Humanistic psychology

> That school of psychology which, in contrast to psychoanalytic and behavioural psychology, emphasises human goodness, potentiality and wholeness. Sometimes called 'third force psychology', humanistic psychology is made up of the approaches of Rogers, Perls, Reich, Moreno, Schutz, Assagioli and others. Humanistic psychology has been called abundance-orientated (positive and forward-looking) rather than deficiency-orientated (preoccupied with pathology). It is inclined towards experiment, co-operation and the stretching of boundaries. It spans therapeutic work from the intrauterine to the spiritual . . .
>
> (Feltham and Dryden 1993: 84)

There now exists a vast range of theories that can be subsumed under the title of humanistic approaches. The following descriptions offer definitions or visions of human beings as proposed by various of the humanistic theories of psychotherapy.

Transactional analysis

Eric Berne (1910–70), despite many years of psychoanalytic training following a medical training, apparently was spurred on to develop transactional analysis in the wake of experiencing very long delays in the assessment of his suitability to become an analyst (Collinson 1984).

Berne's image of the person was, in a sense, contradictory. He saw each person as being capable of being in charge of their own destiny, of almost instinctively wanting to attain (or rather reattain) autonomy – for autonomy is the province of the uncorrupted child before its life is invaded by the 'trash' of negative parental influences. Autonomy, according to Berne (1968) is manifested by the release or recovery of three capacities: awareness, spontaneity and intimacy.

Rational emotive therapy (RET)

Albert Ellis, the founder of RET, developed his approach to therapy through reflection upon and then application of theories of philosophy. Having trained originally within the analytic tradition he is reputed to have been disappointed by the long-term results of his patients (Dryden 1984).

RET holds that humans are essentially hedonistic, their major goals are to stay alive and to pursue happiness efficiently; enlightened by the fact that they live in a social world, they have the capacity to be rational (that which helps them achieve their goals) though they have a tendency towards irrationality. Ellis acknowledges that humans are enormously complex organisms and constantly in flux. Humans can best achieve happiness by pursuing their goals actively.

Personal construct therapy

This distinctive and indeed very scientific approach to psychotherapy was developed by George Kelly who, it is argued by Fransella (1984), was never convinced of the dominant doctrine of behaviourism he first learnt as a student. Interestingly, his first degree was in physics and mathematics before going on to gain a masters degree in educational sociology, a bachelors degree in education and finally a Ph.D. in psychology (Fransella 1984).

His model of the person is thus couched in the language of science, as is his whole theory. His theory, however, is based on the philosophy of constructive alternativism and acknowledges the constant state of motion of both humans and reality.

His model of human beings posits that:

- We are active beings.
- We approach the world not as it is but as it appears to be.
- We approach the world as if we are scientists.
- We have theories about and why things happen, we erect hypotheses derived from these theories and we put them to the test and check their validity.
- We can come to understand ourselves and others in psychological terms through studying the psychological constructs we have evolved in order to help us predict events in our personal worlds.

Fransella (1984) believes that Kelly's work bears a close resemblance to existentialist thinking but notes interestingly that there is no evidence that translations of Sartre or other existentialist writers were available during the period in which he was developing his theories in the United States.

Existential therapy

Existential therapy is still considered by van Deurzen-Smith (1984) to be in its 'early formative stages', having its origins in existential and phenomenological philosophy. Significant thinkers inspiring these philosophies include Kierkegaard, Nietzsche, Husserl, Heidegger, Sartre, Merleau-Ponty and Camus. Early applications of existential theory to psychotherapy were made by Binswanger in Switzerland, Minkowski in France and more recently by Boss (van Duerzen-Smith 1984: 153–4). Indeed, she argues that in the United States Rollo May, Irving Yalom, Carl Rogers, Fritz Perls and Albert Ellis developed certain existential and phenomenological ideas within their therapeutic models.

Existential therapy is thus characterized by the following tenets. Humans define themselves not by essence but by existence: it is only in the way in which I choose my actions and my existence that I define myself as I become. The being of humans is closer to nothingness. It can only come into existence by choosing a particular way to fill the nothingness which exists both inside and outside people.

The tasks we face in life are broadly categorized into our relations with the *Umwelt* (the world around us); the *Mitwelt* (the world with others); the *Eigenwelt* (our own world); the *Uberwelt* (the world above).

However, under normal conditions society encourages the perpetuation of false self-adaptation and therefore of psychological disturbance. Our western economy is based on the craving for falsehood and illusion: machines and appliances, houses and clothes, are overproduced in order to satisfy the urgency of escape from reality. Our task then, as humans, is to face the world with authenticity and relinquish the deceptions of society, to clarify our inner value systems and to come to terms with life by relying on our inner selves.

The person-centred approach

This approach was developed by the late Dr Carl Rogers and emerged from his own clinical experiences, which in his early career had been influenced by analytic thinking as applied to diagnosis and treatment. Both Kirschenbaum (1979) and Thorne (1984) chart the development of Rogers's thinking and formative experiences that led to the significant publication *Client-Centred Therapy* in 1951.

Rogers is perhaps best known for his theory of therapy, which was developed and refined through substantial research, and perhaps less well known for his theory of personality development. A study of these two strands reveals a direct connection between the two.

The single motivating factor in Rogers's theories is the notion of the actualizing tendency (Rogers 1959). All living organisms are subject to this inherent tendency to maintain and enhance their growth. Very early in life human beings develop a self concept which, dependent upon early experiencing, can develop at odds to the overall development of the whole organism. Thus, conflicts arise between the actualizing tendency and the self concept, creating dissonance and disturbance for the person. Rogers's concentration upon the values of acceptance and empathy in therapy directly counters the person's earlier experiencing that has resulted in internalizing external conditions of worth.

Thus, the person-centred therapist starts from the assumption that both they and their client are trustworthy, this trust emanating from the belief in the actualizing tendency and its instinctive movement in humans towards the constructive accomplishment of inherent potential. The therapist's task, then, is to provide the therapeutic conditions for psychological growth, conditions that offer the client the opportunity to review and validate their own experiencing and to move away from dependency upon their internalized beliefs of external values.

An overview and critique emanating from the above models of therapy

In writing this chapter we were struck by the cumulative impact of the cultural values embedded in the wide range of counselling theories we have briefly described. The principal points or cultural beliefs emanating from them are:

- The theories are based on the idea of 'the individual', defined as a belief that individuals are in charge of their own destiny.
- Humans are in a constant state of flux, of movement, of 'becoming'.
- There is a requirement to be active in one's life, not passive.
- The process of growth through therapy is to throw off or shed the effects of parental, family and community influences that have had perceived negative effects.
- The challenge is to live authentically in the social world, to be truly oneself.
- As human beings we have scientific/rational tendencies.
- The world is as we perceive it to be.
- The sanctity of personal authority is not questioned, which implies that:
- All parental and cultural values are open to questioning.
- The concept of personal choice is highly valued.

Several of these themes are gathered within the following quotes from Samuels (1985), who in describing Jung's concept of individuation, states that

> The essence of individuation is the achievement of a personal blend between the collective and universal on the one hand and, on the other, the unique and individual. It is a process, not a state, save for the possibility of regarding death as an ultimate goal, individuation is never completed and remains an ideal concept.
>
> (p. 101).

> Individuation can also be taken to mean 'Being oneself', i.e. who one 'really is', 'achieving one's potential', etc.
>
> (p. 103)

McLeod (1993) acknowledges such culturally determined influences when he writes:

> Freud had lived in a hierarchically organised, class-dominated society, and had written from a world-view immersed in classical scholarship and biological science, informed by a pessimism arising from being a Jew at a time of violent anti-semitism. There were, therefore, themes in his writing that did not sit well with the experience of people in the U.S.A. As a result there emerged in the 1950's a whole series of writers who reinterpreted Freud in terms of their own cultural values . . . Many of the European analysts who went to the U.S.A. . . . were also prominent in reframing psychoanalysis from a wider social and cultural perspective, thus making it more acceptable to an American clientele.
>
> (p. 14)

Our contention is that parallel to the range of individual therapies addressed only too briefly above, the wide range of other therapies that have been developed during recent decades to service couples, families and groups similarly reflects some of the dominant cultural values embedded in American and some specific European cultures.

By contrast with older societies, where there may have been only one form of healing, contemporary society has within it many and varied approaches and practitioners. In part, this huge variety can be seen to be consistent with the ideals of market forces, capitalism and personal choice.

Numerically at the present time by far the greater number of counselling contacts are made through telephone counselling agencies, in situations where the client has much more control over how much he or she is known and how long the session will last (McLeod 1993: 17). This factor again reflects the cultural values depicted above combined with one aspect of widely available modern technology, the telephone. Indeed, as society and science move on, some of the technical developments emerging, for example within computer development and information technology, will mean that newer forms of therapeutic response will have to be developed, as has already been noted through E-mail systems and the internet (Neely 1995). Indeed, the use of technology itself will not reduce or remove the complexity of cultural components, as has been demonstrated already in the field of international telephone and television conferencing.

Whilst it can only be briefly addressed here, Thompson (1992) draws our attention to the ascription of abuse and deprivation, not on to individual clients but on to the very cultural context from which they emanate. In her opinion abuse and deprivation are a holding pattern of our society and culture and are embedded in the collective unconscious. Our culture, itself, therefore has features that are psychonoxious for both families and individuals within it.

Further frequent assumptions of cultural bias in counselling

This heading is slightly altered from the title of an article by Pedersen (1987) where he lists ten frequent assumptions that reflect European and American culture that are embedded in the literature about multicultural counselling and development. These are often presented as if they represent a world norm and certainly do not reflect the numerical reality that many more peoples in the world are in cultures enjoying non-western perspectives.

An examination of the assumptions that underlie our beliefs and practices 'must become an important part of the curriculum in the development of counsellors for a world that includes many cultures' (Pedersen 1987: 17). He lists the ten assumptions as the following:

1 assumptions regarding normal behaviour
2 emphasis on individualism

3 fragmentation by academic discipline
4 a dependence on abstract words
5 overemphasis on independence
6 neglect of clients' support systems
7 dependence on linear thinking
8 a focus on changing the individual, not the system
9 neglect of history
10 dangers of cultural encapsulation.

To a certain extent, the previous section has already addressed points 2, 5, 6 and 8 from Pedersen above. The following paragraphs, therefore, offer partial accounts of Pedersen's other points.

Assumptions regarding normal behaviour

There is an assumption that people all share a common measure of 'normal' behaviour. 'People frequently presume', Pedersen states (1987: 17), 'that when I describe a person's behaviour as 'normal', this judgement is meaningful and implies a particular pattern of behaviours by the normal person.' Implied within this assumption also is that the definition of normal is more or less universal across social, cultural, economic and political backgrounds. Painful experiences of inaccurate diagnosis within psychiatry are reported in Thomas and Sillen (1972).

As Kuhn (1962) pointed out, when a principle of scientific theory has become accepted by society, it functions as a selective screen for defining problems and evidence that coincidentally fit within the scientific principle. Evidence that does not fit the pattern is rejected as irrelevant or too chaotic to consider. Society is thus protected from reality by the fixed form of abstract principles. Research data itself becomes something used to defend abstractions that posit stereotypes and inaccurate generalizations about normality. Quite obviously, what is considered normal behaviour will change according to culture, context, situation, who is judging and why and so on.

Fragmentation by academic discipline

Pedersen here is referring to the complexity and variety of theoretical frameworks that exist for different professionals, whether they are doctors, theologians, sociologists, counsellors and so on. Such frameworks not only define clients' difficulties differently but, moreover, subframeworks exist within each discipline. Seldom do helpers exchange insights, information or questions between the disciplines as they should.

Further, the client with their problems does not necessarily fit into these artificial constructs and, indeed, they may actually confront directly the professional's beliefs about them and the helping method.

Dependence on abstract words

Quoting Hall (1976), Pedersen introduces the concept of high and low context cultures. In a high context culture, people search for and expect meaning to be embedded in the context of different situations. Low context cultures, on the other hand, relate concepts of meaning to words and phrases. Western cultures, within Hall's theoretical framework, are low context and as such there has been a considerable development of abstract words and concepts within many disciplines. Such abstractions are often difficult, if not impossible to comprehend if one has originated from outside of this culture.

Dependence on linear thinking

Linear thinking is described as the process whereby each cause has an effect and each effect is tied to a cause. The assumption is that everyone depends on this causative relationship.

'How then can counsellors adapt counselling to a cultural context', Pedersen asks (1987: 21), 'where the cause and the effect are seen as two aspects of the same undifferentiated reality (as in the concept of Yin and Yang) with neither cause nor effect being separate from the other? Some cultures describe events as being independent of their relationship to surrounding, preceding or consequent events.

Neglect of history

History has an appropriate relevance for a proper understanding of contemporary events. Many counselling approaches focus on the present even when some of the client data is based upon their own past. Counsellors, Pedersen suggests, are much less likely to attend to clients who talk about the history of their people. (Examples of this would include clients' stories of forebears, ancestors, religions, ethnic and tribal history and so on.) In many cultures the connection between past and present history makes it necessary for counsellors to understand clearly the client's historical context as a way of understanding their present behaviour.

Pedersen, of course, is writing from an American background, acknowledging that counselling is a young profession in a young country. He suggests that counsellors, therefore, are less conscious of history than those who belong to nations with longer traditions. In the UK there is a slightly different combination of these two factors: counselling is a much younger profession than in the US and yet Britain has a long and complex history. This combination would be interesting to research in terms of its effects within therapy.

Pedersen believes that not only do counsellors lack a sufficient awareness of the ways in which people solved their problems over the previous thousands of years, they also lack the patience for a longer perspective in which the current situation may be transitional. Lacking respect for tried and tested ways in which a particular culture has dealt with personal problems, the preference or tendency will be towards trying out the latest trend or fad in counselling methods.

Dangers of cultural encapsulation

The final assumption that Pedersen offers is that counsellors already know of their assumptions! Within a multicultural/multiracial society, and as a consequence the counselling setting, counsellors need to recognize the danger of any closed, biased and culturally encapsulating system that promotes domination by an elitist group. If counsellors are unwilling to challenge their own assumptions they will be less likely to communicate effectively with persons of different cultural backgrounds.

Brief reflections on and of western therapists

In a fascinating penultimate chapter of their edited book *On Becoming a Psychotherapist*, Dryden and Spurling (1989) present their analysis of the preceding ten chapters written by eminent psychotherapists from different theoretical backgrounds. The chapters offer personal and often moving accounts of some of the motivating experiences that contributed to their wishes to become psychotherapists.

A recurring theme in the writings of several of the therapists was that of the experience of being a 'stranger' or 'outsider' (p. 196). Many childhood experiences were recounted in which the combination of observing others in distress, feeling for them and a desire for intimacy featured. Often these experiences had led to a need to understand the nature of relationships. Several also discussed the experience of deeply understanding or knowing what others were going through as if their empathic qualities were already highly tuned. Some of these dimensions were construed as coming together in the practice of therapy as a form of detached intimacy.

Considerable emphasis was also placed upon the 'being' of the therapists and that this was construed to be as important as the doing, in relation to the clients. Images, perhaps, of the wounded healer abound here, as does the idea propounded by Dryden and Spurling of the self standing for the imprinting of theory. 'The language of the self is an expression of the need for theory in psychotherapy to be impure' (p. 207). The personality of the therapists and the extreme difficulties of fully explaining what happens in psychotherapy lend to this impurity.

Dryden and Spurling quote Chertok (1984) in considering the phenomenon of the relationship between client and therapist which runs through the history of psychotherapy:

> This relationship has taken many different forms and been called various things down through the ages: Mesmeric fluid, suggestion, transference, empathy, symbiosis and so on. But the fact is inescapable that, in spite of its long history, we still know very little about it.
>
> (Dryden and Spurling 1989: 209)

Many of the writers used metaphoric concepts such as process, rhythm, dance, journey in attempting to describe their work. Interestingly, it was also noted how psychotherapeutic language borrows and transposes ideas, ways of thinking, and metaphors from other traditions of thought, e.g. religion, politics and from the narrative tradition. This apparent openness to other influences and systems of thought bodes well for therapists who are sincere in getting to grips with the challenge of understanding culturally different clients and their own systems of thought.

The nature of persons who become psychotherapists is extremely fascinating, as presented by this evidence, and further complicates the relationship between theory, practice and culture as embedded in the persona of the counsellor.

The above, all too brief information suggests that those who become therapists are potentially persons who have striven to understand the difficulties that have beset their lives, have had the capacity of being emotionally in tune with others, have also experienced their own distance or alienation from others and who have attempted to transpose those experiences into a constructive helping mode, that of being a psychotherapist.

As a link to the next chapter it seems appropriate here to quote from Victor Turner, an anthropologist, who is describing a shaman in a traditional society (cited in Dryden and Spurling 1989). His description, perhaps, could be attributed to many psychotherapists today.

> In many ways, he was typical of Nolembu doctors: capable, charismatic, authoritative, but excluded from secular office for a variety of reasons, some structural, some personal. He was the typical 'outsider' who achieves status in the ritual realm in compensation for this exclusion from authority in the political realm.
>
> (Turner 1967: 371)

7

Non-western approaches to helping

A white woman kneels in the centre of a hardened cow-dung floor, surrounded by 100 or more Zulus. The Zulus wear an assortment of beads and animal skins, and they are dancing to an incessant drum beat which reverberates around the grass and mud hut. The woman is about 30 years old and is looking nervously at a white goat held upright in front of her by a couple of black youths. They spread open its legs as a razor-sharp short spear, an assegai, is pressed against the animal's belly. The goat lets out a terrified scream. A murmur of approval goes up from the spectators.

The assegai is plunged into the beast's heart, killing it swiftly. The woman bends down and puts her lips to the wound; the blood trickles down her chin. During the week this woman works as a state prosecutor. Today, in this remote 'kraal' in the rolling hills of Zululand, she has just completed her initiations as a witch doctor'.

(Hobbs 1993: 20)

Introduction

The ways people cope, attempt to solve their problems and seek assistance are shaped by the social and cultural norms and the symbolic meaning within their culture. Further, several authors have pointed out that differences do exist between cultures on what is even deemed as problematic. (Torrey 1972; Yui 1978; Herr 1987; Westwood 1990).

Five principles have been identified by Torrey (1972) as crucial to successful helping in any culture. These are:

- The client's problem is named.
- The personal qualities of the counsellor are extremely important.
- The client's specific expectations must be met.
- The counsellor must establish credibility through the use of symbols, skill or power.
- The counsellor must apply certain techniques designed to bring about relief to the troubled client.

An immensely useful model of contextualizing healing activities is provided by Tseng and Hsu (1979) who assert that 'in all cultures at all times

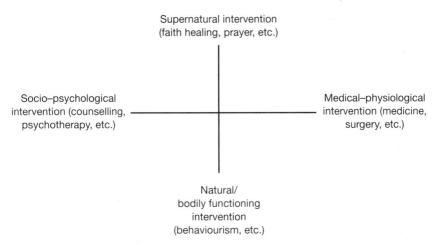

Figure 7.1   Four healing interventions with their consequent methodologies

there have been four dominant modes of healing' (see Figure 7.1 and also Figures 1.1 and 1.2)

The matrix depicts four major areas of concern and activity involved in the healing/helping process. In traditional healing practices healers have often worked in and with all four domains with their troubled 'clients'. We could imagine, then, a situation in which such a healer would listen and talk to the troubled person (socio-psychological), might prescribe medicines, lotions etc. (medical-physiological), recommend or instruct the client towards certain behaviours (natural bodily functioning), and pray or engage in spiritual ceremonies seeking divine blessing (supernatural intervention).

By contrast to the above very inclusive healing model, the western development of expertise (where specialists concentrate upon more discrete areas of activity) has led to the separation of the four domains depicted above into medicine, priesthood, behaviourism and counselling/psychotherapy. From this perspective we gain an overview that indicates the relative impoverishment of the separation of any one healing form from the others as compared to traditional practices. According to this model a counsellor, a doctor, a priest or a behaviourist is only each addressing one quarter of the healing spectrum! A further complexity is that a multitude of theories of counselling and psychotherapy now exist (481 named theories according to Karasu et al. 1984). Therefore, in one quarter alone of the above healing matrix, there are over 400 approaches!

Though a little dated, the views of Torrey (1972) still seem to be relevant, where he asserts that western trained helping personnel (psychiatrists, social workers and trained counsellors) are socialized to see alternate forms of helping as inferior to their own. Such attitudes in the professional domain might mean that practitioners not only fail to respect other healers but also do not consult, refer to or indeed work in association with other healers on their clients' behalf. If we are truly concerned with maximizing the potential for helping culturally different clients, and we know that those clients are also consulting different practitioners, it seems incumbent upon us to support the belief systems and self-healing impetus of clients by being open to other healing approaches.

Philosophic assumptions underlying world views

In an important article that asserts the importance of understanding the philosophic assumptions underlying world views, (the deep structures of culture, as Jackson and Meadows 1991 term them), three sets of hypotheses are offered for understanding European, Asian and African conceptual systems of culture.

The *European* system emphasizes a material ontology, with the highest value (axiology) placed on the acquisition of objects. External knowledge is assumed to be the basis of all knowledge (epistemology), and one knows through counting and measuring. The logic of this conceptual system is dichotomous (either–or), and the process is technology (all sets are repeatable and reproducible). The consequence of this conceptual system is an identity and self-worth that is based on external criteria (e.g. how one looks, what one owns, prestige and status symbols) (Myers 1988).

The *Asian* conceptual system emphasizes an ontology of cosmic unity, with the highest value (axiology) on the cohesiveness of the group. Internal and external knowledge is assumed to be the basis of all knowledge (epistemology) and is an integration of mind, body, and spirit, which is considered to be three parts of the same thing (Cox 1988). The logic of this conceptual system is *nyaya* (a unity of thought and mind) and the process is cosmology (all sets are independently interrelated in the harmony of the universe). The consequence of this conceptual system is an identity and self-worth based on being and on an internal and external reality.

The *African* conceptual system emphasizes both a spiritual and material ontology with the highest value (axiology) on interpersonal relationships between women and men. Self-knowledge is assumed to be the basis of all knowledge (epistemology), one knows through symbolic imagery and rhythm. Therefore, the primary emphasis of the counselling pair should be building the relationship and recognizing the importance of the knowledge that the client has within himself or herself. The logic of this conceptual system is based on co-unity, and the process is that all sets are interrelated through human and spiritual networks. The consequence of this conceptual system is an identity and self-worth that is intrinsic.

The above underlying systems of cultural assumptions will inevitably be embedded within the indigenous healing systems of those cultures. Let us now look rather more specifically at some different approaches.

An overview of various treatment methods

In an attempt to review models of helping in non-western countries Lee et al. (1992) received completed questionnaires from professionals working in mental health and related areas in seven countries (Barbados, Korea, Nigeria, Pakistan, Singapore, Sudan and Zambia).

Three categories of assumptions about the causes of psychological distress and behavioural deviance in these countries were reported: family dynamics, fate and possession by evil spirits.

This study also revealed that two indigenous models of helping seemed to be pervasive. These are described as 'kinship systems' and 'spiritualism-religion'. Within the first category of kinship systems the evidence suggested that the family plays the most significant role in the resolution of mental health problems. An underlying notion seems to be that the whole family shares the problem and suffers with the individual, and it is the family that will help the disturbed individual.

In many of the countries surveyed a great deal of stigma and shame was attached to mental illness; as a consequence it was only when the problem could not be contained that family members would seek other forms of help, often from within the extended family.

Beyond the family system community members also offer an abundance of support to troubled individuals. An example is given from Nigeria where large assemblies of 'clansmen' are brought together and are presented with an individual's problem. A group effort is then involved to solve the problem. Additionally friendship was also noted as an important therapeutic tool, with friends becoming involved in the helping process.

The other dominant form of approach to helping that featured in this survey, that of 'spiritualism-religion', is a key element, also, in the various specific methods described later in the chapter. By contrast, western theories of counselling and psychotherapy have become secularized from religious beliefs and do not, in themselves, address this aspect of life, let alone use teachings or rituals from within a religious perspective.

In writing the previous sentence we are aware of being dangerously simplistic. There are western theories of therapy that do acknowledge the importance of spirituality (e.g. transpersonal, Jungian, psychosynthesis) but these tend to be in the minority in relation to the large number of therapies quoted in Chapter 6.

Great importance was placed by the respondents to the study by Lee et al. (1992) upon traditional healers, who were identified by a variety of names such as shamans, medicine men, piris, fakirs, black magic experts, hakeem, motwaas, alfa and Sufis. Shamans tend to operate by entering an altered state of consciousness to contact and use an ordinarily hidden reality to acquire knowledge, power and to help others (Harner 1990).

Medicine men were reported as being popular and widespread in Brazil, Senegal, Nigeria, Zambia and Korea, prescribing herbs and other traditional medicines for both mental and physical illnesses.

The piris and fakirs, mentioned above, are religious men of the Muslim faith (reported in Pakistan and Sudan) who use verses of the Koran in different ways to treat mental illness.

The report revealed that black magic experts were also found in rural areas of Pakistan, claiming to have extraordinary powers that they can use to either help or harm others. Conceptualizing diagnosis in terms of evil spirits, such practitioners would often provide weekly visits and offer special magic words for the individual to wear or keep in their room to ward off the spells.

The hakeem are traditional healers from Saudi Arabia who are generally found in small villages. They are called on to deal with various illnesses and their methods include dietary therapy and the use of coal on the nerves, each hakeem also being described as having their own specialization.

Motwaas are religious men also found in Saudi Arabia. They cite verses from the Koran and prescribe herbs to treat the mentally ill.

Alfas are Nigerian spiritualists. There seems to be a trend in Nigeria to go to spiritual churches or religious healing houses in cases of distress. Alfas are the spiritualists in these traditional healing houses.

Recognition is made by Lee et al. (1992) of the tendency for these traditional systems to be more popular in rural areas in these countries rather than in urban communities – though even in urban areas there are reports of people being treated unsuccessfully by western adopted methods and reverting to traditional systems of belief for cure. Personally (and culturally) held systems of belief in relation to the cure of ills are obviously profoundly embedded in the individual and the collective psyche. Such belief systems cannot be easily accounted for and overcome by western technology as the parallel example of research into the surprising effectiveness of some placebo treatments in western countries powerfully indicate (Park and Covi 1965; Frank 1973).

Sufism

'Muslim Sufis' major role all over the world is to provide succour or relief to persons in distress and pain.' This is the opening sentence of Kemal's (1994: 87) article explaining the Sufi tradition and from which the following details are taken.

There are several steps in the Sufi helping process, often carried out in *khangahs* or seminaries, where the Sufis abide. The first step, after having been given food and shelter is to see if there is something there in the seminary to meet the troubled person's interest.

The second step is to form a contact with the 'master' (this title is applicable to both genders) which gives the person with the problem an opportunity to speak their mind. They can either be specific in defining their problem or they can talk at length giving vent to their hurt and pain. This may be in one sitting or continue over a period. In this process the master Sufi tries to 'understand the person's problems and the person within him.' Once it becomes clear to the master what the problem basically is, the next step is to find out whether the person has the ability to see the conflict and resolve it.

There is an entire collection of Sufi literature (stories, parables, anecdotes, sayings) which can be used for the individual's help, to enable them to see the light. Through literature, the client is given enough information and facts that help him/her identify his/her own problem. As in any other form of counselling or analysis, the ability to see the truth and accept it takes time.

The next step is to give the individual a wider perspective and a broader idea of the role of human beings in the universe so that they can see their own role.

What the *khangah* does is to give the individual support and acceptance until the conflict or the influences of the society and the system are understood and they gain enough insight to face life and their role in it, with the proviso of returning to the *khangah* should they so wish. Sufis also encourage the use of mystic and meditation exercises.

In Sufi terms, the individual, through various exercises, is allowed to experience ascension of arc – in the mystic terms known as initiation, meditation, invocation, contemplation and actualization.

Knowledge according to the Sufis has three aspects: knowledge through communication, knowledge through observation and knowledge through experience.

Sufism, as described above, offers a combination of nurture within residential settings, significant attention from a healer, the use of historical collected wisdoms, and meditation exercises embedded within a religion/philosophic system that embraces a view of the world and humans within it.

The healing processes of the !Kung hunter-gatherers

A study of !Kung healing may suggest principles fundamental to human healing and development, shedding light on their origins and evolution.
(Katz 1989: 208)

The following information is taken from the chapter by Richard Katz in Colleen Ward's (1989) collection of essays on altered states of consciousness.

Among the !Kung hunter-gatherers of the Kalahari Desert, healing is a central community ritual with significance far beyond effecting a cure.' Katz proposes a definition of healing based on his anthropological work with this group as 'a process of transitioning towards meaning, balance, connectedness and wholeness' (p. 207).

The healer serves as a vehicle to channel healing to individuals and the community, without accumulating power for personal use. As an aside, it is worth noting here that contemporary professional codes of ethics also embody this important principle.

The primary ritual among the !Kung, the all-night healing dance (which can happen as often as four times a month) epitomizes characteristics of sharing and egalitarianism, strong concepts in !Kung life. The healing power, or *n/um* is the most valued resource at the dance (and one of the most valued resources in all community life).

As the healing dance intensifies, *n/um* (energy) is activated in those who are healers, most of whom are among the dancers. As *n/um* increases in the healers, they experience *!Kia* (a form of enhanced consciousness) during which they heal everyone at the dance. The intensified experience of *!Kia* (when the *n/um* has risen up and awoken the healer's heart) leads to an altered state of perception that facilitates a process of 'seeing properly', a capacity that allows the healer to locate and diagnose the sickness in a person. Sickness is then pulled out as healers bring their vibrating hands close to or in contact with a person. The healers are putting their *n/um* into the other person and at the same time pulling the sickness out of the other and into their own bodies. This is difficult, painful work. The sickness is then expelled from the healer.

Fiercely egalitarian, the !Kung do not allow *n/um* to be controlled by a few religious specialists, but wish it to be spread widely among the group. All young boys and most young girls seek to become healers. By the time they reach adulthood more than half the men and 10 per cent of the women have become healers. *N/um*, an unlimited energy, cannot be hoarded by any one person.

A public routine cultural event to which all have access, the healing dance establishes community; it is the community, in its activation of *n/um*, that heals and is healed.

The therapeutic use of altered states of consciousness in contemporary North American Indian dance ceremonials

The above title is that used by Wolfgang Jilek (1989) in his exposition of three different dance ceremonials in the edited book by Colleen Ward (1989). The following information describes the major elements identified in these rituals.

Salish spirit dancing

The winter spirit dances are the major ritual activity of the Salishan-speaking Indians of the Pacific coast of North America. While much of Salish Indian culture crumbled, the ceremonial was performed clandestinely by older people, despite efforts by government, churches and school authorities to suppress this 'pagan' ritual in the last century. Spirit dancing was openly revived in the 1960s.

Today, in the revived ceremonial, the initiation itself is the way to acquire power for self-healing. The major purpose of the initiation process now is to cure serious psychosomatic, psychosocial behavioural disturbances of young Salish Indian people who are seen as suffering from spirit illness due to alienation from traditional 'Indian ways'. Salish ritualists consider American Indian persons suffering from depression, anxiety and somatic complaints that are unresponsive to western treatment – as well as young Amerindians with behavioural, alcohol and drug problems – as candidates for spirit dance initiation.

The death and rebirth myth is the central theme of the collective suggestions surrounding the spirit-dance initiation. According to contemporary Salish theory, it is the spirit power that acts through the initiator on the initiates, and it is this spirit power, not the initiator, that cures the novices, burying their ailments and conflicts together with the old personality and at the same time giving them rebirth into a new life.

A threee-stage process of this therapeutic approach is discerned by Jilek and described as (1) depatterning through shock treatment, followed by (2) physical training and (3) indoctrination.

The various stages of the initiation process are as follows. First, initiates are kept in a dark cubicle or 'smokehouse tent' within a longhouse for a period of usually ten days during which time they are called and treated as 'babies'. They are bathed, fed, dressed and constantly attended by babysitters. Regression is thus imposed on the initiates, who are reduced to a state of complete infantile dependency. Within the uterine shelter of the darkened longhouse they hatch their power and prepare to grow with it into a more rewarding and healthier existence.

Through the four days of the depatterning process the initiates are blindfolded, are subject to repeated and prolonged treatment of bodily seizure, immobilization of limbs, hitting, biting, tickling, subjection to kinetic stimulation (whirled about, lifting and dropping, etc.) and intensive acoustic stimulation (loud drumming, rapid rhythms, etc.). Initiates are also starved and fluid intake is restricted.

Then follows a phase of physical training which is associated with intense indoctrination and is 'supposed to make the baby strong'. Long runs, often in snow, and cold water swims, constitute the main activities of this phase.

Running in the longhouse is accompanied by drumming and chanting and clapping of the crowd.

Released from their incubation the initiates 'feel their newly acquired power wherein the song bursts forth from them and these leaping steps of their first dance carry them through the longhouse' (Jilek 1989: 170).

Jilek's analysis of the drumming rhythms of the Salish spirit dance reveals that the frequency cycles used are consistent with frequencies occurring in ceremonies associated with trance behaviour, which are to be effective in the production of trance states. Jilek concludes that this ceremony combines the following therapeutic modes:

- occupational/activity therapy
- group therapy
- cathartic abreaction
- psychodrama
- direct ego support.

The Sioux sun dance

This sun dance originated with the plains Algonquins around 1700. By the 1800s it had become the most magnificent ceremony of this culture, involving complex group rites associated with mythological themes revolving around war and the bison hunt. Officially banned by the authorities, the dance ceremonial was changed into a therapeutic instrument dealing with health and community problems that directly or indirectly were to do with the white intrusion.

The sun dance has the characteristic features of shamanic initiation: calling and instruction by dream visions; guidance and teaching by a shaman; ordeal experience with fasting, thirst, pain and privation; and finally questing for and receiving a personal vision in the last dance.

The gourd dance

Modern gourd dancing has developed its own characteristic choreography. Historically embedded in the traditional societies of the plains and prairie tribes, the 1960s and 1970s saw enthusiastic adherents carrying the dance from its origins in Oklahoma to plains and prairie tribes throughout the USA and Canada.

The classical plains Indian style of gourd dance, popularized by the media, appeals to the younger generation of Amerindians from diverse reservation backgrounds who strive to move beyond a tribal identity towards a Pan-Indian identity. Participants see in the gourd dance a recognized means of experiencing their American identity and a way of changing their life to a more wholesome existence. The dance has considerable ego-strengthening and rehabilitation potential and the therapeutic effects account for its success as a popular movement among rural and urban Amerindian populations.

Mediums in Brazil

This section is based on Stanley Krippner's chapter on 'A call to heal: Entry patterns in Brazilian mediumship' in Ward (1989).

In early African cultures, as in many traditional cultures today, an individual was seen as being intimately connected to nature and the social group (Katz in Ward 1989). As an aside, this assertion is categorically opposite to the predominant values in many western countries today, particularly the UK, North America and Australia, where individuals are connected more to technology and the pursuit of individualism. Connections to the social group are considered to be weakening and some writers have urged that more focus is required by therapists on small- and large-group work to reawaken this vital human element of relatedness (De Marré 1975; Lago 1994; Samuels 1993).

Returning, however, to these early African cultures, each individual was thought to be part of a web of kinship relations, existing only in relationship to the larger family and community networks. Strained or broken social relations were the major cause of disease; anger, jealousy and envy could lead to serious illness. A harmonious relationship with one's community was necessary for health; the relationships one's ancestors had with the community were also important. At the same time an ordered relationship with the forces of nature was essential for mastering the well-being of the individual and community. Long before western medicine recognized the fact, African traditional healers had taken the position that ecology and interpersonal relations affected people's health (Raboteau 1986).

The medium, or person through whom the spirits spoke, achieved a trance state brought about by dancing, singing and drumming in order for incorporation to occur (the voluntary surrender of mind and body to the discarnate entity). Treatment for afflicted people included herbal preparations, prayers and sacrifices. It frequently included spirit incorporation. Preventive medicine consisted of using charms and rituals as well as living within the social constraints of one's culture.

Of the Brazilian spiritistic movements, Candomble is the one most closely resembling the pure Yoruba religion of Africa and retaining the original beliefs and rituals. The majority of healers are women though in some regions there are men. Aside from learning how to sing, drum and dance, the novices also learn about the herbs and special teas and potions given to troubled members of the community.

Other Brazilian spiritistic groups include Kardecismo, which is a spiritistic movement (dating from *circa* 1818) organized around the principles of homeopathy. Kardecist mediums alter their consciousness usually by 'turning inward' (often aided by soft music and the presence of a supportive social group) and providing an 'opening' for the incorporation of their guide.

Another group, Umbanda, has a name which seems to have come from the Sanskrit term *Aum-bandha*, the divine principle. Alterations of consciousness in the 'low' Umbanda sects may be facilitated by drumming, chanting, smoking cigars, drinking rum, making sacrifices of fowl and small animals and drawing cabbalistic signs on the floor with chalk. 'High' Umbanda sects do not engage in these practices but use trance-induction methods reminiscent of Kardecismo. Both groups emphasize the importance of spirit incorporation and all Umbandistas venerate Jesus Christ.

There are also other less popular spiritist groups (e.g. Batugur, Cabock, Quimbanda, Macumba, Xango).

All the ceremonies of the three major groups vary, yet they share three beliefs: humans have a physical and a spiritual body; discarnate spirits are in constant contact with the physical world; humans can learn how to incorporate spirits for the purpose of healing.

The use of trance states depicted in the last three examples (the hunter-gatherers, the native American dances and the Brazilian mediums point us to the importance of this form of healing. As Wittkower (1970: 160) has written:

> There can be no doubt in anybody's mind that trance and possession states in the countries in which they play a part of religious rituals have an important distress-relieving, integrative, adaptive function. As far as mental illness is concerned, they may be of prophylactic value. An increase in mental illness may have to be expected when as a result of culture change they have ceased to exist.

Spiritual influences on healing among Afro-Caribbean groups

In a book entitled *Working with West Indian Families*, written from an American perspective, Gopaul-McNicol (1993: 103) suggests that:

> One reason West Indians have not fully accepted the concept of psychotherapy is that their approach to solving problems is internally orientated. Problems are kept within the family and solved there. The only outsiders who are permitted to intrude are priests or ministers and the church's role is basically one of providing emotional support and reaffirming the family's belief that God will solve this problem in the right time. Some families in distress may consult spiritists. Such 'Obeah'

practitioners are believed to be able to control evil spirits which tend to be perceived as the causes of family troubles.

She goes on to suggest that:

> If an individual or family problem is not seen as a medical one, then it is usually categorized as a spiritual one. In such cases West Indian clients first go, not to a mental health professional but to an Obeah practitioner (a spiritist or person who practices witchcraft) or a member of the clergy. The Obeah practitioner takes into account various aspects of the family situation, such as recent success and failures: puts them in the context of the cultural beliefs in spirits; and works out a plan of action according to his/her conclusions.
>
> (p. 111)

The healing of an individual normally takes place in a group ceremony known as a seance (although it can be done individually as well). The group usually comprises junior spiritual leaders, family and friends. The Obeah practitioner who serves as a medium attempts to establish contact with the spirit world in order to determine which evil spirits are creating the person's dysfunction and which good spirits can be enlisted to protect the person. An attempt is made to convince the evil spirits they should 'do good' rather than 'do evil'. The practitioner will then interpret the spirits' messages for the family and will prescribe medicinal herbs, ointments, spiritual baths, prayers and/or massages, all with the goal of helping the individual gain spiritual strength.

Chinese psychiatry

In an interesting chapter on Chinese psychiatry, Wen-Shing Tseng offers an account of a system of mental health practice that combines Chinese tradition with contemporary interpretations and western modes of treatment (W.S. Tseng 1986: 275). 'Chinese medicine', he writes, 'especially psychiatry, has been relatively less influenced by religious thoughts and movements throughout the course of history.' The study of medical textbooks reveals that the theoretical system of Chinese medicine as a whole is 'nature'-orientated and is based primarily on the concept of yin and yang, the theory of five elements and the idea of correspondence between microcosm and macrocosm. Such a theoretical orientation also applies to psychiatry. The cause of mental disorders is attributed to natural factors, psychological stimulation and the individual's own attributes.

The influence of emotional factors upon the occurrence of physical illness has long been recognized in Chinese medicine; the improvement of the emotional condition is emphasized as a way of encouraging recovery (Chen 1963). Chinese medicine in actual practice is very much orientated to the prescription of herbal medicines. More than 400 types of material from vegetable, animal and mineral sources are frequently used in traditional medicine. Among these nearly 100 are used in the treatment of psychiatric disorders.

Present practices in China follow a number of different approaches:

- Community psychiatric services – mental health delivery systems follow the government's four main principles of health: (1) primary concern for labourers, farmers and soldiers; (2) emphasis on prevention; (3) the combined use of Chinese traditional medicine and western medicine; and (4) the combining of mental health work with mass movements. Care in the community occurs where patients' families, neighbours and retired workers assist in the care of patients. It usually takes two or three people as a team to take care of one patient. This team observes the patient's condition, supervises the taking of medication, provides guidance and education and assists the patient in socio-family rehabilitation.
- A combination of traditional and modern medicines – Chinese medicine uses traditional herbal medications, acupuncture, and western methods including ECT.
- The predominance of biological descriptive orientation (influenced by traditional approaches to medicine) – relatively scant attention is paid to sociocultural and psychological aspects of mental health and illness, not to mention the emphasis on the dynamic orientation of human behaviour, mind and psychopathology evidenced in some American textbooks. A predominance of biological descriptions of mental ill-health pervade the literature.

Given the shortages of mental health workers and the widespread diagnosis of certain forms of mental ill-health (e.g. neurasthenia – not a diagnosis often used in the west) the Chinese developed an 'accelerated – integrated therapy' for treating such patients. The emphasis of this treatment was to integrate all available modes of treatment to deal with the patients as a group and to accelerate the pace of treatment within a short period of time, usually several weeks.

The treatment programme took several forms:

- group therapy, with an emphasis on educating patients about their disorders
- the reforming of life patterns, with an emphasis on physical activities and intellectual encouragement
- adjunctive somatic treatment of various kinds including medication, acupuncture, etc.

Summing up

In reflecting on three major studies (two in the USA, one in the UK) that explored the nature of people's religious experiences, Valla and Prince (in

Ward 1989) note that all three surveys indicate that some 20 to 40 per cent of the population report mystical or religious experiences and that such experiences (in the USA surveys) were more commonly reported by blacks than whites. Two of the studies found that frequent experiences were connected with higher social class; the remaining survey found the reverse.

Valla and Prince note that healers around the world have shaped and developed 'spontaneous experiences' (as explored in the surveys reported above) to arrive at highly elaborated healing systems. Meditation traditions, drum and dance-related trance-inducing systems and healing practices employing psychedelic drugs are well-known examples.

In attempting to make comparisons between western therapies and the wide range of material presented in this chapter, it seems crucial to note that, at a basic level, we are not comparing like with like. Most western therapies have an individual emphasis, others described here have a community or family focus. Most western therapies are delivered in a one-to-one setting, others described here may use several healers who may work in group settings. Most western therapies do not involve friends or family members in the therapeutic process. They do not induce, deliberately, altered states of consciousness through ritual dancing or chanting. However, writers such as Rogers (1980) and Wood (1990) acknowledge that clients and therapists may experience altered forms of consciousness in the therapeutic process.

In short, the western concepts of psychotherapy – though having a broadly similar aim to many other culturally different healing forms – focus on individual interactive processes most frequently based in dialogue.

However, there are many contradictions to the above assertion. There are western therapeutic methods that use behavioural approaches, use creative activities (movement, dance, sound, art), involve meditative processes (relaxation, stress reduction), respect and work with metaphysical and spiritual issues, have systems of befriending (e.g. alcoholics anonymous), work with families, small and medium groups and so on.

We have to recognize the breadth and complexity of this spectrum of healing approaches embedded in all societies and note that each has its validity within the cultural frameworks from which it originates. In addition, there are often similarities between the forms of activity used by different cultures, e.g. trance states, though the rituals may be differently structured.

All the healing systems described in this chapter are certainly community- or communally based, i.e. they involve numbers of people. But so too, does western psychiatry, where doctors and nurses and occupational therapists are all involved. However, at the other end of this western spectrum is the example of isolated people, living on their own who consult individual private therapists on an hourly basis once a week. The therapist seldom addresses the needs for others to be involved, and indeed there may be no convenient other person. The client may be very anxious about such initiatives occurring until they themselves are ready to embark on such socializing.

In short, any simplistic comparisons with other therapeutic forms are doomed to failure. Therapists are urged, however, to respect and to take very seriously their culturally different clients' wishes and views in relation to what they conceive as helpful. A preparedness to attempt to accept other healing perspectives and approaches, even when not understanding them, is crucial. One's task, where there are apparently competing healing systems within the client's frame of reference, seems to be to effect, as much as possible, a way of working that encourages the client in their help-seeking mode, and to explore methods of cooperation with other helpers.

8

Filmed cases: training aids to the therapeutic process

I've come to make a complaint really. Because I'm starting a job next week. I've got a child of three, so I went to see this childminder in my area and I asked her if she would look after my child; it was a white lady and she just looked at me and said 'We don't take black children', and slammed the door in my face'.

I've come to see you, perhaps because I think I'm pregnant. I don't know what to do. I mean, me being an Indian girl and pregnant, my mum's gonna kill me, my dad will murder me. Oh, I'm in such a situation. If only I had something I could do about it, I don't want an abortion because I don't believe in them, I don't think they're right. Oh, but maybe that's the only way I can get out of it.

(transcripts from Clark and Lago 1981)

Introduction

The intention of this chapter is to offer a series of transcripts of short interviews, involving the use of counselling skills, between same race and crossrace pairings of counsellor and client. Following each transcript there is a short discussion which explains further the dimensions and complexities of the phenomena of race and culture manifested in the interviews.

The use and value of filmed material has long been recognized in counsellor training. The supply of this material to training courses was originally provided by Keele University Careers and Counselling Unit, who ran a film lending library featuring a range of American therapists working with clients and with groups. This complete library was later purchased by the British Association for Counselling, who in recent years have passed over the administration of it to Concorde Films. In the intervening years technology has changed considerably; the original 16 mm spools of film requiring cine-projectors have been replaced by videotapes and video-cassette recorders.

Of significance in the world of counselling and filming has been the pioneering work of the late Dr Norman Kagan on a system that eventually became known as interpersonal process recall. Kagan and his colleagues were able, through the extensive analysis of filmed helping interviews, to identify certain response modes used by counsellors that were consistently helpful to clients. In recognizing, also, that each person in a helping role is differently affected by how 'helpees' present themselves (verbally, physically and emotionally) they derived an interactive technique of using film with training groups to enable trainees to explore their own affective responses to a wide range of interpersonal challenges. Finally, Kagan and his associates refined their methodology to include also a structured system for using audio and video recordings of meetings (counselling interviews, committee meetings, class teaching, etc.) as a mechanism for reflection upon and supervision of such sessions.

The second example of Kagan's major contributions referred to above, that of interactive film, became the stimulus and model for the development of an early video training programme entitled 'Multi-racial videoscenes'. Developed by Jean Clark and Colin Lago at De Montfort University, Leicester, this short programme consisted of 16 short vignettes in which people from a range of different cultural and racial backgrounds speak directly to the camera about a troubling incident or emotional situation. Two examples are given as opening quotations to this chapter. The training group are invited to consider their affective and verbal responses to these potential 'client' statements, having been asked to imagine that they are the counsellor or helper to whom the person on screen is talking. Such apparently simple stimuli have generated substantial discussion among groups of practitioners from different helping professions on a range of different matters:

- What would I feel if I had a client presenting these issues to me?
- How would I respond to the client and their issues?
- Would my feeling and verbal responses be congruent with each other or quite different?
- What assumptions are raised in me by the scene?
- If I were in such a situation as the client, how would I react?
- Why do other colleagues in this training group react similarly or differently to me?
- What are the issues there that I may learn from?

It can be seen from the above that interactive film techniques have substantial value as a counselling training medium. Stimulated by both Kagan's original idea and the success of 'Multi-racial videoscenes', a series of other interactive videos were made during the early 1980s to stimulate training in areas such as working with international students, racism in the church, and working in multicultural and multiracial organizations (see the appendix at the end of this chapter).

Recognizing the enormous training potential of film and videos and the paucity of existing materials on this subject, the authors collaborated on a further video project in association with University of Leicester entitled 'Issues of race and culture in counselling settings'.

'Issues of race and culture in counselling settings': a video training programme

This video and training manual are available for hire or sale from the University of Leicester Audio Visual Services.

The video contains six scenes (four of which are presented here) involving counsellors and clients from same-race and different-race backgrounds. The participants shown in the video were friends and colleagues of the producers and have actively been involved in the work of the RACE division of the British Association for Counselling.

Each of the scenes depicted lasts approximately ten minutes and there was no editing of these interviews. The participants (when acting as clients) were invited to present a concern that was legitimate to their own personal, cultural and racial backgrounds. No scripts were offered or written. Each participant in the video is featured twice, once as a counsellor and once as a client. As counsellors, the participants were invited to respond as they would in their normal counselling mode. When the video is shown in training situations trainers are recommended:

- to show the introduction
- to have previewed the videotape and read the manual beforehand
- to have chosen the specific scenes they wish to use for this training session
- to show each chosen scene, one at a time (not sequentially) and
- after each scene to offer time for the training group to reflect and discuss on the proceedings.

The introductory notes and transcripts of these interviews now follow. After each script there are a set of questions which readers may think about in order to explore further their own ideas and responses to the presented scripts.

Readers should remember that the following transcripts are taken directly from the video, verbatim, and thus should bear in mind that considerable differences exist between the spoken and written word. Live conversations are aided by all sorts of other non-verbal and paralinguistic cues which are obviously absent in the written form. Some of the following sentences, therefore, in the transcripts convey meanings that are not readily clear.

Interview 1: Josna and Terri (A black client with a white therapist)

Spoken introduction

This scene shows the client exercising her right to feel trusting of her counsellor. In the past she has had experience of working with white colleagues which did not lead to very satisfactory outcomes. In all counselling relationships the process of establishing trust between client and counsellor is crucial. This task might take much longer when those involved are from different cultural and racial backgrounds than it would with people of the same race, and the process may also need to be much more explicit.

Further background thoughts

The following scene could be experienced as a threatening situation for the therapist depending on his/her level of knowledge, experience and awareness of, and comfort with the issues of race and culture.

In this scene the questions posed by the client in order for her to make an informed choice are very explicit. It is important to stress and realize that in many similar situations the client's questions may not be verbalized in such an explicit manner, but we suggest that nevertheless such questions and quandaries may be present in the client's mind and their experience: even if they are not verbalized, the helper cannot afford to ignore them. Our suggestion is that it would be useful for the therapist to check out if such questions are present. We realize, however, that for many therapists and trainers who have not yet been exposed to the issues of race and culture, little awareness or knowledge may exist that such dilemmas abound and are of great importance to the client.

The transcript of the interview follows; this is followed by a series of questions that may be helpful in contributing to the group's discussion.

Transcript of the interview

Terri: Josna, do you want to tell me why it is you would like to talk to me?

Josna: Before I start talking to you about something that is disturbing me a lot, I feel I need to know a bit more about you. I just got your name from the telephone directory and I don't know anything about you. I just would like to know a bit more about you before I can really talk to you. Have you done any work with black people?

Terri: Yes I have. Let me just tell you a little bit. My original training was in nursing and I have completed a two-year diploma in counselling skills in London. Which is in fact, a mixed-race course where there are black and white people on the course. As part of my practice I do work with people from all backgrounds and also people with disabilities. So people can be black, white, Asian and also can have a disability and I work from home. I also train and I do some training in race and culture with a black colleague. I have been doing this for several years now.

Josna: The course that you were talking about, besides having black people in the course itself, in terms of the training element, did it have any training on race?

Terri: No. When I started my course in 1977, we were probably one of the beginning courses that were beginning to really be aware of the issue of race and culture and the need to understand more. But there certainly wasn't any training. This was 1977 to 79.

Certainly now, in courses that I run I won't work the course around that course. I usually prefer to do the work with a black colleague so that at least that issue is addressed, and as part of my aims and objectives with people it is stated very clearly that issues of race, colour and language are addressed in the context of my work and for students to own that there are concerns and that certainly as a white woman I own that I am racist and that I need to keep looking at that and need to keep reminding myself.

Josna: How do you deal with the question of race on the courses that you are running?

Terri: I almost want to say head on; by actually making sure that it is overt and not covert and if there is a language that is used and if it is subtle – things like 'well we feel like that don't we?'. It's almost like nudging people to collude. And being aware of words that people will use, of being aware of the need to put in things like roots and origins exercises into things that I run.

I have a sense, I feel, we have slightly reversed role. I don't mind being asked but I would also like to know a bit about you as well. I feel I have said things that will help me to understand some of what it is you are really asking me.

Josna: Well, it is just that I have worked with white people. I do work with white people at a professional level and am very aware of the racism that they operate with. I just refuse to be placed in those situations that are going to undermine me. As your client I don't want to receive any racism from you. That is why it is really important for me to check you out. That is what I am doing and I want to know how you operate.

Terri: One of my responses when you say you don't want to receive any racism from me is I am aware I am racist. There are times I may be that way and I would hope, because part of my commitment, if I am to work with you, would be that you would also challenge me as I would enable you to work through whatever the issues were. As far as I know, I am not blatantly racist and, yes, there are times when I get stuck like anybody else and get caught. Hopefully, I am aware enough that I will own that and that I will actually come back to you and say 'look I was reflecting on this and I felt that how I put something across to you was racist'. That is all I can say to you. That is difficult because I don't know in what area other white people, maybe other white women, have been racist to you and how they have used their power. For me, in working with you as a client it is about an empowering and an equal relationship. I am into equality. How does that seem to you?

Josna: I feel that you have given me the right answers and I have had all the right answers from white people before – at the intellectual level – and I don't trust all of that, I have to tell you. I do know that if I do decide to have counselling from you and enter into a therapeutic relationship with you that it will be a risk and I will have to see how it goes. For me, it is a big risk and I am not avoiding issues as I try to clarify these very important concerns for me. It is not a block to what the real anxiety may be about. I just feel that it is like buying a house which may look very attractive and solid and it is important to get the structural survey done.

Terri: It sounds like you have been around this way before and have been hurt, that you have actually tried to enter into a contract of looking at issues that are around for you and it has been rather difficult and you have not got what you wanted out of it. Has that only happened with a white person or has that happened with other people?

Josna: I haven't entered a therapeutic relationship. I work with people. I have worked with a lot of people. I have got a lot of experience with working with people as colleagues and have worked together from different areas. I have no problems on a common point of contact. All of that has taught me that these people appear to be working in the interest of black women and sisterhood are really about a different world completely. It is from those work experiences, and I have seen how counsellors have worked with women that I know, I suppose I am very cautious, I don't want to be treated in that way.

Terri: Your analogy of buying a house and having the survey done – there are so many different types of surveys – you don't know until you have taken the risk to buy. It's like this is what I hear you trying to check out with me. Do I want to buy this commodity you've got? All I can say to you is, what I sense from you, is yes I would like to work with you and I feel it is worthwhile you taking the risk to work with me and should issues come up then we look at those and also look at how they are affecting your life as an Asian woman working with Asian people, with white people, and it's risky. I have the same risk with you. It's not just one sided.

Josna: I'm sure. I know of one therapist who works with quite a lot of black women and has written a book about black women without even getting their permission and writing for them. How do I know that you are not going to use what I say?

Terri: What I do is set up a contract of confidentiality. I do have a supervisor where I take issues that come out of therapy sessions to them, that it remains within the context of you and I, and my supervisor. It is a held confidentiality. It is about trust. That is it and it's you taking a risk on it. It's difficult and I appreciate that. I can feel you are kind of 'how do I know?'. You don't know. That is the problem and I really do appreciate what you are saying. It's like 'Am I really going to put myself into this position, with you as a white woman, Terri, how's it going to be?' I don't know.

Suggested questions

1 Does the client have a right to check out the therapist before making a commitment?
2 How confident is the therapist in being open to questions from the client?
3 In such circumstances how do you feel you would respond?
4 How much information does the therapist need to give to the client to help contribute towards a trusting relationship?
5 How is trust established between client and therapist?
6 Can you identify the range of issues in this scene beyond that of establishing trust?
7 If you felt threatened or inadequate by the client / by the client's questions what would you do?
   (a)   refer the client elsewhere?
   (b)   take it to supervision?
   (c)   gain extra training?
   (d)   what else?

Interview 2: Belinda and Stan (a white client with a black therapist)

Spoken introduction

This scene gives the opportunity to continue to explore these major issues on race, sexism and power which are inherent in counselling situations between people of different races.

Belinda starts by discussing her predicament of being a white female manager of a team of people from mixed racial and cultural backgrounds.

Further background thoughts

In situations such as these the task for the therapist is very complex and it is difficult to identify where the focus should be. Not only may the therapist be required to understand the client's projections but he/she has to cope with his/her own fantasies about the client's projections and meanwhile attempt to stay open and receptive to what the client is bringing.

It is important to respect the enormous risk faced by the client in bringing these issues into the counselling setting especially when the therapist is so clearly identifiable as a member of the (complained about) racial group.

An added dimension in this scene is the theoretical framework from which this therapist practices. Coming from a background of reevaluation cocounselling his style may be unfamiliar to many but nevertheless is consistent within that theoretical framework.

This scene highlighted in the transcript below can evoke strong reactions for training groups and consists of a wealth of issues for exploration and discussion.

Transcript of the interview

Belinda: The issue that's around for me really is about my relationships with people at work, particularly since I've been promoted into a managerial post as a white woman manager. The issue particularly causing me most concern is about my relationships with black men in the institution. Which is about me as a woman and me as a manager. There are kinds of dual issues there. My problem is that I really don't know how to sort those things out and I don't know what they are about, just that they cause me a lot of anxiety and I'm not handling them very well and taking them all in on myself because I don't know what to do with them so I'm here to talk to you about them.

Stan: What have you done so far?

Belinda: What I have done so far is to talk to the other white women who are managers in the same place as me and checked with them whether they are feeling the same things as I am and what they are saying is that they are not.

Stan: How does that feel for you?

Belinda: It made me feel pretty angry actually because I find it difficult to accept that they don't feel anything, that it's not an issue for them. When for me, as a white person in a managerial post it has to be an issue. But I suppose where this one is different is the fact that there is the issue of gender as well as power in a formal sense. The other thing that I have tried to do is to broach the subject and talk about it with some of the individual men concerned but I felt very vulnerable about that because it felt like me pushing my problem back on to them because I feel it is my problem to sort out, what is my racism in it anyway, in order to be able to talk about the sexism that I feel coming from them towards me.

Stan: So what have you come up with so far in thinking about it?

Belinda: What I have come up so far with is the fact that as a manager I see myself as managing people and it's about my relationships with people that that's what makes the organization tick and for them what I am as a manager is somebody who has a particular hat on, that I should be using my hat. There is a much more strictly defined view of what a manager is that I have.

Stan: Is it a question of can you as a manager be a person as well?

Belinda: Yes and I feel that I still am a person but the person isn't having much of an outlet at the moment.

Stan: What's in the way?

Belinda: What gets in the way is different things. Shall I give you an example? I was walking across the corridor yesterday and one of the black teachers came up to me and said 'Belinda, I want to go on a course. Here's the stuff. Will you go away and do it for me?' and I went 'Yes. OK. Sure.' The mixed feelings about that for me were yes, I feel flattered that I've been asked, that I'm trusted enough to go away and people know that I will follow things through and I won't let them down and I will deliver the goods. But what wasn't nice was that I almost felt dehumanized, like a machine, I'm this manager and dump it on to me, she'll do it. There was no negotiation around it. That was the problem for me that I felt I had no choice, that that's my job, that's what I have to do and it wasn't a kind of person-to-person relationship.

Stan: What would you like to have said given those thoughts and feelings you had?

Belinda: What I said was 'Yes, fine, sure, of course I will' and went away. What came up was 'God, I wish I had said, do you want to talk about it, let's have a look at what the course is, what do you want out of it, and just made it more of a person-to-person thing. I felt very oppressed – woman go away and prepare the dinner, woman go away and do this for me. That's what it felt like. And I wanted to say 'Hang on a minute, what's happening? Why are you doing this to me?' but that wouldn't have been fair.

Stan: You are a woman, you are a person, you are a manager, so what can you do?

Belinda: What can I do?

Stan: What actually stops you from asserting yourself as a woman in that situation?

Belinda: It's a kind of benevolent, womanly, motherly feeling really, in that I feel I must meet people's needs because they are always telling me nobody else does and they can't trust other people so there is quite a lot of pressure on me not to repeat the same things other people do and not to let them down, or to not hear them or whatever. But in the meantime, I feel that I'm not being heard, that I am disappearing in all of this and running around picking up pieces and doing things. And I feel very servile and what's stopping me is not wanting to disappoint them and not wanting to be accused of being a racist. The sort of games other people play but in a different way. So it's my own fear.

Stan: So what do you want for you?

Belinda: What I want is, I want to have relationships which recognize that despite the fact that I am a manager, I am a woman, I am a person and I'm not just a thing that's there to get things done and to make sure things run smoothly and that I need some support too.

(short silence)

Stan: What's that thought?

Belinda: What's that thought? I just have this image of myself as an object that things get fed into and things come out the other end, a bit like a sausage factory I suppose and I'm the factory and stuff comes in and stuff goes out and that the real me is lost.

Stan: If you weren't being careful, given that image that you have just presented, what would you say or do, if you weren't being careful when that happened to you?

Belinda: I suppose that's the dangerous bit because what I want to do is turn and say 'you fucking bastard, leave me alone, why are you doing this to me? I'm really oppressed by this.' And that frightens me when that kind of notion of 'you bastard' comes up because what's next to that is 'you black bastard' and that's really kind of difficult for me to cope with because I kind of hate it because it is recognizing that it is within me still, despite the kind of intellectual things I might have about racism, the fact that that can come up, not often, but when it does, it's really shocking and it adds to my feelings of guilt that I could easily be another of those people in management who repeats the same patterns and does the same things. I feel that I am overcompensating all the time and I'm shocked that that is within me. And I find it really hard to deal with and that is my problem.

Stan: What are your thoughts now?

Belinda: My thoughts are it's happening to me now. I feel really ashamed that I said the words 'black bastard'.

Stan: What does it feel like?

Belinda: Horrible. It feels really degrading to think like that and to know that it's there and that I can say it in front of you. It's really hard to accept it of myself.

Stan: What I want to give you, I think it's really important right now in this situation, that you actually own that. I think that's really what needs to happen and I really am pleased that you have actually found that it's been possible even to say that because in order to shift whatever needs to shift, these things need to be faced. And I am really, really pleased that you said what you said because it's important, it's not nothing, it's real and it's there.

I have another question. If this were an ideal world how would you alter the situation that you're in to make it right for all the people concerned? First thought?

Belinda: I was thinking that I would have enforced support groups where people would be able to talk about things openly and honestly and be able to express their feelings openly. Because I think even in an ideal world people would have negative feelings about each other, whether they were based on race or gender or whatever it was. And that people could work together to solve the issues that are between them and that is what isn't happening for me now I suppose.

Stan: So, what would get in the way of you actually setting that up?

Belinda: What has got in the way of me setting that up, because I have tried to do that, and then allowed myself to get pushed back into not doing it, is feeling that I don't share a language with people to talk about issues, or people saying 'that's not a problem for me' or 'I don't see it like that' because I have to deal with it in an all white group, I don't feel it's fair to push more of my racism and my problems on to black people, but finding other white people who are willing to go through that process and talk things through is hard. It may not be in other parts of the country, but it feels like it is here.

Stan: So what are you left with?

Belinda: Feelings of aloneness a lot of the time. Books to read. Developing friendships with black people that help me to be aware of what feelings come up through those friendships. But then I have to go somewhere else to deal with those feelings and not to the people concerned.

Stan: Do you have the space to go and do this?

Belinda: Not as much as I need.

Stan: Is it possible for you to set that up more?

Belinda: I feel it has to become a priority, it's about the priority which I have given it, which is probably not as much as it needs to have.

Suggested questions

1 What are the issues here? (A brainstorm to begin your consideration might be helpful.)
2 How important is it to have knowledge of different theoretical frameworks in order to appreciate and understand different styles of working?
3 What stereotypes may be present in this scene?
4 What is your reaction to the following statement as it relates to this scene? 'The presenting problems that the client brings to this relationship seem to parallel, or are reflected in, this therapeutic alliance.'
5 To what extent do personal values influence the therapeutic relationship?

Interview 3: Stan and Julia

Spoken introduction

Stan and Julia are both of African Caribbean origin. Here the issues are about race and gender and about self-worth and self-esteem. Stan discusses his relationships with black women and how they see him. He does not want to be stereotyped.

Further background thoughts

Common stereotypes that are present in our society have the capacity to block us from communicating effectively with persons of those stereotyped cultural and racial groups. A black male in this position may therefore experience how difficult it is for his openness and honesty in expressing his concerns to be understood for what they are, outside of his own racial and cultural groups. Not only has he got this to cope with but he is actually complaining about experiencing the oppression from women in his own racial group.

Forces and levels of oppression are complex phenomena in society and become internalized in people. Consequently their effect can be to distance people one from another even in the same racial group, though originally the oppression may have emanated from outside of that racial group. The following scene offers an opportunity to examine further how individual perceptions may affect attitudes and behaviour.

Transcript of the interview

Stan: What I want to say is how difficult I find it in really knowing that there are black women here for me. What I find is there is a tendency for them to dismiss me as a black man. And what I want to say is don't give up on me. Don't give up on me. I am a human being too. What I want from you is the highest expectations of me. And to bear with it because it is not easy. It's not easy for me as black man struggling in this particular society, against all the things that are put on me as a black man. One of the ways I need to feel OK is to know that there are black women there for me. That's what's really hard. I feel as though I am not even listened to.

Julia: What happens to you when you feel you are not being listened to?

Stan: Well, a whole lot of things come up for me around questioning me and the whole question of whether I am black or not. Which may seem really strange. I've just got to look at myself in the mirror and it's quite clear. But there's a lot of stuff that goes on around who's black and who's not, who's really black and who's not and it just begins to highlight all that stuff and I begin to feel I'm not the real McCoy. It hurts. It really hurts. That's what comes up.

I think I've worked quite hard trying to just recognize that whatever my experience has been, OK, so I was brought up here in this country and spent many years of my life growing up amongst white people, not having any black friends. I've worked quite hard to recognize that that experience is a unique experience, it's real and it's also part of my experience as a black man. But then when I get these things happening to me where I feel as though I am being dismissed, it feeds right into that stuff, into my insecurity and I just feel that I want to go away.

Julia: Cruel in some ways.

Stan: Well, I just feel completely isolated. I feel even more isolated. Isolation runs for me a lot. One of the ways that I go is just to isolate myself and that can happen in many ways.

Julia: How would you do that? If you were going to isolate yourself how would you do that?

Stan: One way is just to physically remove myself from the situation. Another way is just to go quiet. Those are two quite obvious ways.

Julia: You've mentioned about expectations, about wanting me to have high expectations of you or from you, what does that do for you?

Stan: Well, I think I am thinking about black men generally. It's about expecting, not in the kind of pressured way, but expecting that I can achieve, that I am all the best that you can possibly imagine a man to be, but that's possible and that can happen with me and not just to dismiss me and say it's never going to happen. That I'll never get anywhere. That I'm rubbish. It feels like I'm rubbished. It's about having high expectations and even though you can actually see me struggling, to see the struggle and to support me in the struggle, rather than give up and say 'Oh no, it's not going to happen, what's the point', or giving up yourself.

Julia: I have a sense of, what comes out for me is wanting to be validated, a sense of validation and a sense of actually seeing you as a person with what it is you have to offer, rather than just totally dismissing what you have.

Stan: I think also what happens, it feels like I get put with all other men. That all men are the same. So there is no point in even really paying attention to what this man is going to say. And that is really hurtful. I think it's hurtful not only for me but for all men. It doesn't make us feel good, it doesn't make me feel good. There is something in that about not recognizing me because I am just being put over there – 'Oh, you're a man and you're a black man, so you're there.' And what I am saying is 'see me'. That's what I want.

Julia: If black women were to see you, what would they be seeing?

Stan: They would be really proud if they really saw me.

Julia: Tell me a bit about that.

Stan: I think what they would see is someone who really does care a lot about the world and the way the world is and cares about trying to get things right and tries in the things that I do in my life, to do that, to bring about the changes that I want. I try to live up to my ideals and I am proud of me. I do respect myself a lot. I like myself. I think that's very important and I still am able to respect and like myself despite all the stuff that gets put on me. I think I am very powerful.

Julia: The theme is about validating, seeing you for what you are, not actually taking you for granted or making assumptions about you and about men in general. To me, there's a sense of a bit of a dilemma that goes on as well. The fact that you are a man and that within that there are other things, the image, the person that you are.

Stan: I suppose there is something about sexism that comes out. The fear that the sexism will come running up between us – me as a black man and you as a black woman or any woman. I suppose people make mistakes, people do things, and I suppose what I sense is a fear around the whole area. I think what I am trying to say is I really feel that I have actually worked quite a lot, I'm not saying that I am sexist, around my own sexism and it gets hurtful when I get a sense that I am being dismissed because I am a man and because I am a sexist and I think what needs to happen is, yes, we need to be sensitive to what goes on, and we will make mistakes, but that is learning and it just feels . . . I'm not sure what else to say really!

It feels like there is only one statement, that I really want to say is 'don't give up on me'. There's another bit as well that says 'love me'. I think that's really important.

Suggested questions

1 What is your reaction to the client's presentation of his concern?
2 What is your reaction to the interaction between the therapist and the client?
3 How sensitive is the therapist to the issues being experienced by the client?
4 What value would you place on same-race counselling pairings in view of the issue under discussion?
5 By contrast with the above same-race pairing, what different effects on outcome might there be if the counsellor was of a different gender, racial or cultural origin?

Interview 4: Rani and Josna (client and counsellor both of Asian origin)

Spoken introduction

This vignette features a counsellor and a client who are from similar race and language backgrounds. The scene raises questions about how far counsellors with similar cultural, language and racial backgrounds to their clients are more able to be of help to them.

Further background and thoughts

Despite the apparent similarities of race, culture and language of the participants in the following scene, recognition has to be made of differences that exist between the therapist and the client which might include aspects such as difference in age, the effects of western acculturation and the relative importance of returning to one's roots.

The phenomenon of age can play a significant part in relationships in certain cultures. Certain roles might only be fulfilled by persons of specific ages.

The effects of western acculturation can introduce other dilemmas for persons of non-western background. Not only do they have to deal with the issues as experienced in their own culture, they also have to face the issues that are prevalent in the host culture. The two sets of realities described above can conflict with deep-rooted individual values and beliefs and create much confusion and anxiety for those experiencing them.

The deep yearning for one's roots is not only a profoundly worrying experience for individuals but seems to be an archetypal need in that it seems to affect humans whatever their countries of origin.

As this scene demonstrates, not only are the above issues present but the value of a shared language is also made explicit.

Transcript of the interview

Rani: I've decided to come and see you because for the last year or so I have been very depressed and there isn't any reason to be depressed. I have been going to my doctor and saying that I'm not well. My family are getting fed up because I am not very happy but they don't know why and the doctors said it might be a marital problem and sent me to a marriage guidance counsellor and I got very fed up with her because she just kept on sitting there and saying 'hmmm, hmmm', and that didn't help me at all. So I thought I would come to see you. Maybe you would be able to tell me what I should do?

It's not a problem. It's not a marital problem. I just feel that I want to leave this country, go back. [She continues in Hindi]. It is as if my heart has left this place. [She returns to English]

I just can't feel that I can continue to live here, get old here, see what they do to the old people here. And I think if I fell sick, and I am alone, I haven't got a husband now, I've got a son who has become very westernized and I worry about this all the time. And there is all the time this question in my mind 'Where shall I go?', "Where do you belong?', 'What am I doing?'. I feel very happy here, when I am working and everything is fine. I've got very many English friends. I like living with them. I like my friends. I like the country. But at the same time there is something in the back of my mind which continuously says 'You don't belong here – go back home.' And I did go back home. I went to India and then I found that I didn't fit in there. Now I feel very lost and have become depressed. I thought maybe an Indian counsellor would help me and particularly sort this out for me about what to do.

Josna: Right, I just want to say that there are lots of difficulties that you are experiencing and certainly I would be happy to explore these with you. I don't think I would be very happy to tell you what to do.

Rani: Then what is the difference between coming to you and going to an English counsellor? I've been there and she keeps on talking about this could be something to do with middle age, this could be menopause, this could be . . . I know all that. What I really want to know is . . .

Josna: [in Hindi] Your heart has gone away from this place . . .

Rani: . . . and I want to know from another Indian – do you feel like that? Is it something just with me? When I talk to my English friends they say but you have done so well here, you are like one of us and should be happy here. None of that sort of feels [right], as if they don't understand what I am talking about. I seem to have lost that kind of a contact and I feel a little lost. This was my focus for coming here when we could sit and explore all that, but I really need to have somewhere where I can go and feel I can get some answers.

Josna: What sort of answers are you looking for?

Rani: Whether what I feel is common with immigrants. Whether it is not just something with me? Is it me who is going sick? Does this happen to all of us when we leave our own countries? You see I don't have anyone else to chat this out with because I live in a little town, there are not very many Indians there and I haven't got contact with my own community. And I feel now terribly isolated and terribly lost and yet I have lived in the same place for 20 years, I know lots of people there. So there is quite a lot of, you know, like anxiety which floats around in my head and in my mind. I can't put my finger on it. What is it that I'm so worried about? What is it I don't like? [in Hindi]. It is as if . . . [English] some of the things that I think about. Sugar cane doesn't grow in this country. Mangoes don't grow in this country. They are alien to this country. In the same way, we can't put our roots here. These things which we have grown up with. So I sometimes feel that what we are trying to do here is unnatural, artificial and that we have transplanted ourselves and sooner or later we begin to grow sick. These are the sort of thoughts that are constantly floating around in my mind.

Josna: [in Gujerati] You feel you cannot grow in this country, there is no sunshine here.

Rani: [in Hindi] No, no.

Josna: [in Gujerati] And for these reasons you feel great sorrow and you are very alone.

Rani: [in Hindi] Yes, absolutely alone . . . So what do you think I should do?

Josna: [in English] You are not alone in what you are going through. There are other women that are going through similar things.

Rani: Are there any groups I can go to?

Josna: There's a group of Asian women who are going through similar isolation. It is a self-help group which meets regularly at the Centre and they talk about their different experiences and offer support to each other within the group and also outside.

Rani: What will I expect from them? What will they be able to give?

Josna: I think what most of the women go to the group for is to know that they are not on their own.

Rani: You see I am not on my own.

Josna: In their experiences of isolation.

Rani: When I meet my relatives at weddings, nobody admits that. They all show on the surface tremendous success. They talk about their children at university and how much money they have made. Everybody looks very successful and very happy and then you have a little group every time you meet, we sit there and say 'Where shall we go next?' 'Which country shall we go to?' It's as if we have all become gypsies. There is nowhere where we say 'This is it, this is home, we settle down here.' I think in our case by constantly saying we will go home once we have done this, once we have finished our education, we haven't let our children settle and I feel a tremendous sense of perhaps guilt, in first uprooting everybody and going abroad and then constantly talking about what has been left behind and then now being in this kind of dilemma which I can't talk very much about because it would cause so much stress to everybody around me. So, I have got to make up my mind and I find it very hard to do so. I still don't know what it is that I will have to do or what it is that has caused so much stress.

Josna: How long have you been feeling like this?

Rani: For quite a long while now. Off and on I think for the last few years. I think when we first came here there was so much struggle in trying to make a living, trying to make a home. I think now that everything is there. We have a nice home. There is enough money. There isn't that anxiety about earning a living. The day-to-day worries are finished and I sometimes feel that, when you sit down to take stock, and you suddenly feel that you have been struggling and struggling and now that you have reached somewhere it is no longer what you want or what you were running around madly before. And I think it is like a sense of anticlimax, of disappointment. I find I have no one to check this out with.

Josna: When you check out people . . . ?

Rani: Everything is fine. And when I talk to my English friends they give the superficial answers like 'you've done so well' and 'you don't suffer from any discrimination: why are you feeling like this?'; 'Perhaps you should start dating; you should have started seeing other people.' It's like this is incomprehensible to them. My Indian friends don't tell me this. I think they are so busy denying that there is any feeling of being uprooted that they don't want to admit it.

Josna: How do you feel about joining a group of women that are sharing openly?

Rani: I'm not sure.

Suggested questions

1 Consider the relative values and dangers of therapists having more than one language.
2 How helpful would it be to you to have an understanding of the cultural norms and role expectations of your client's culture.
3 What do you value about your own roots and origins?
4 Apart from the readily identifiable issues, what other factors might influence the counselling relationship?
5 What may have been the client's expectations of this helping process?
6 What other issues emanating from her own background and identity might the counsellor have been conscious of in her attempts to help this client?

Appendix to Chapter 8

The following videos are used in counselling training about multicultural and multiracial issues:

'Hear and now: working with overseas students'. Producers: J. Clark and A. Parker. United Kingdom Council for Overseas Students Affairs (1982).

'On stony ground: a sequence to help you explore thoughts and feelings about race'. Producers: J. Clark and C. Roberts. Produced for Leicester Diocesan Council for Race and Community Relations by the University of Leicester, Audio Visual Services (1982).

'Through one thousand pairs of eyes'. Institute of Education, London University (*circa* 1983).

'Multi-racial videoscenes'. Producers: J. Clark and C.O. Lago. Leicester Polytechnic, Department of Educational Technology (1981).

'Issues of race and culture in counselling settings'. Producers C.O. Lago and J. Thompson. University of Leicester, Department of Audio Visual Services (1989a).

—9—

Addressing the context of the counselling organization

> I define culture as the collective mental programming of a people . . . it has become crystalised in the institutions these people have built together: their family structures, educational structures, religous organisations, law, literature, settlement patterns, buildings . . .
>
> (Hofstede 1980)

Introduction

This chapter, like the previous one, concentrates upon the practical applications of counselling and, more specifically, upon the overall context within which it is delivered. Historically, the literature on transcultural counselling has substantially ignored organizational and systemic issues (Bachner and Rudy 1989). However, they may be the very issues that affect the outcome of the therapy for better or worse. Consequently these dimensions cannot afford to be neglected. The suggestions contained in the following text are directly linked to and influenced by much of the theoretical material introduced in the previous chapters.

The nature of the organizational context within which counselling takes place is crucial in providing a conducive and therapeutic setting for clients. Hall's (1976) attention to context and its relationship to meaning (that has been previously discussed in Chapters 4 and 6) further reinforces our view that the location within which the therapy takes place might be for some clients as important as the therapy itself. The association between place and meaning may be much closer in some cultures than others, though even within a 'low context' culture such as Britain, the psychological association of churches with worship, surgeries with medicine, schools with learning and so on is a close one. Words such as ambience or atmosphere are regularly attributed to particular settings or buildings by visitors who feel themselves to be affected by the surroundings. Our intention here is to stimulate organizational thinking on the nature and decoration of buildings and the provision of internal systems that constitute the very context within which the practice of therapy takes place.

In acknowledging this potential power of surroundings upon people's emotional states, it would appear woefully negligent, indeed anti-therapeutic, not to attend to these matters in any counselling setting, let alone one with a specific remit of offering a transcultural service. Architectural and visual symbols communicate data to clients and have a power, therefore, to represent the values of the organization. The following short sections provide some of the dimensions worthy of consideration in designing an atmospherically conducive counselling organization.

Location of counselling agency

Self-evidently the location of the organization needs to be directly related to the proposed clientele that it aspires to work with and on behalf of. This statement does not imply that this is a simple task to achieve. For example, an agency might 'set up shop' or be offered premises on a busy street, between local shops, in the commercial and social heart of a local community. By contrast, premises might be offered or located some considerable distance from the community the agency hopes to serve.

In the first instance, are potential clients likely to feel able to walk in if they are fearing that they may be seen by neighbours who are out shopping? How acceptable (within the local culture) is the activity of 'going for counselling?'.

In the second scenario, how easily accessible is the building from the community it is intended to serve? What are the local public transport service facilities like? Has the building got its own car park or are there transport facilities close by? Could clients afford the travel costs? If the agency is open in the evenings, is access considered to be safe in relation to street lighting and proximity of transport?

Both discretion and convenience of access are important considerations. As shown in Chapter 7, mental ill-health and psychological distress are sources of fear, shame and embarrassment in some cultures. It seems prudent, therefore, to anticipate this issue in determining where the agency is to be located. A generally useful operating principle might be to seek a building that is sufficiently close to the community it serves to afford reasonably convenient access and that is close to but not in the centre of the community and its 'trade routes' of pedestrian and motorized traffic. All of the above also relate to the importance of disabled access. Gates, narrow footpaths, steps, may all prove formidable barriers to reaching even the front door of the building. If the agency is also located on the second or third floor and there is no lift access, what chance do disabled people have of getting there?

A further consideration here will be the proximity of the agency to countertherapeutic facilities. For example, a counselling service geared to assisting alcoholics might not wish to be next door to an off-licence or pub; similarly a service concerned with helping sexually abused people might not want to be sited close to a sex shop or cinema showing 'adult' films. Though these examples seem far-fetched, one does come across such scenarios in reality. A less extreme but as terrifyingly frightening for clients was an example, some years ago, of a counselling service in a school where not only was the counsellor's office next to the headteacher's but that the headteacher involved insisted she interview all the children before they saw the counsellor! The result was obvious. No effective counselling occurred.

The use of signs and name plates are also of concern. How are potential clients going to know that they have arrived in the right place or what the functions of the agency are?

The design, details given and positioning of the sign boards and name plates on the building thus have to be presented clearly. How much information is required? This might vary from a minimum of a very clearly visible street number on or near the front door, if clients have been referred or directed, to much fuller descriptions detailing name, address, purpose, hours of opening, instructions for leaving messages, named personnel and so on. If the agency is located up a side street or contained within rooms within a bigger building, additional signposting giving directions might also be worthy of consideration. To have an appointment and then not be able to locate the agency easily and conveniently could be a source of great distress to new clients.

An agency local to one of the authors has a discreet name plate, bell push and invitation to enter. The agency is situated in a terraced house and the front door may be opened leading directly into a waiting room. Once there, an internal door, which is kept locked, has instructions for the user and a bell push to signal the client's arrival and bring the receptionist to the door. Clients do not, therefore, have to wait outside on the street to be let in.

Increasingly, public buildings in cities employ a security system whereby the front door is kept locked and access is granted by using the bell push and announcing your arrival to the receptionist through an intercom who then lets you in. Again, what effects might this have upon an already anxious client who also might fear being seen waiting on this specific doorstep? Similarly, agencies may have to consider how they might enhance the sensitivity of general portering and reception staff who are servicing 'customer' enquiries in larger buildings accommodating different organizations.

The overall ethos of this and some of the later sections is to urge a consideration of the psychological importance of orientation, induction and transition upon clients.

The psychological research and literature upon transitional periods in our lives (e.g. going away to university, starting a new job, getting married, suffering bereavement, hospitalization, going on holiday, emigrating, etc.) highlights the significant effects of change upon our normal emotional functioning. Though one would hope that approaching a counselling agency in itself is not a traumatic transition, it certainly can be so for many. Additionally, clients will already be distressed for that is the very reason they are coming. Consequently, an important task to be considered by an agency is that of how to facilitate the clients' easy access into the counselling process through the appropriate consideration of location, signposting and entry procedures detailed above.

Publicity and other literature

The processes of orientation and induction of clients into the counselling process inevitably begin at the client's first awareness of the organization's existence. This knowledge may come from friends' conversations, local gossip, mention by referring agencies and available literature distributed by the counselling organization itself. Not all of this information may be conducive or indeed accurate. However, the counselling organization does have more direct control of its literature and may use this to good effect if it is designed and edited well.

Prior, clear and accurate information helps the client prepare for their initial contact. Beyond details of location, hours of opening, charges etc. opportunities also exist for describing the procedures of what might happen when a client approaches the service, how the counselling process is conducted, what problems might be helped and other details. In a certain sense, this orientating function of the agency's literature is also an aid to acculturation into the counselling process.

Attention must also be given to the importance both of the nature of language used in these documents as well as which languages are featured. The former will determine the extent to which professional or technical language is used and the clarity with which it is presented. Which languages to use will, of course, be determined directly by those languages spoken by the community it is hoped to serve.

Internal décor and style

We now move our attention from the outside of the building to the interior. We have already discussed the possibility of access and ease of movement for the client from the street into the building. The quality of reception, as shown both by the décor as well as the receptionist, will have significant impact upon the client and their sense of comfort in this new situation.

All cultures have conventions related to hospitality. These conventions influence both design and layout of buildings as well as informing interpersonal behaviours. This whole chapter is concerned with stimulating a consideration of how counselling organizations can create the conditions (physical, psychological and emotional) within which successful therapy can occur. In attempting to ease the transition of the client from the outer world to their inner world, counselling personnel will need to consider the impact of the environment and interview rooms as well as their own modes of greeting the client. This factor applies to the reception staff who often do not get help, support or guidance on their task, a task which is so vital to enabling the successful transition from street to therapy. Special courses for the reception staff and involving them in staff meetings can be useful mechanisms for enhancing their knowledge and improving practice.

Achieving a balance between suitable formal surroundings consistent with public service and providing a more intimate and culturally appropriate setting is a considerable challenge to those staff charged with the interior design. Many features of the reception area and interview rooms will require consideration and are listed below for convenience and clarity:

- colour and design of wall covering (paint, wallpaper) and complementary colours of ceilings/woodwork
- use of floor coverings/carpets/tiles, etc.
- furniture – style, comfort, conducive layout
- visual images – posters, calendars, paintings, statues, models, icons, notices
- plants and fresh flowers
- lighting – electric, candles, central, bright, dimmed, sidelights, etc.
- location and storage of leaflets and other information
- heating – source of, fireplace, radiators, etc.
- smell – wood polish, neutral, incense, fresh air spray, pot-pourri, etc.
- availability of refreshments – water, orange, tea, coffee, biscuits (or not)
- convenient and signed access to toilets.
- The reception desk needs to be protected or regularly monitored to ensure that any confidential material is not easily exposed to clients. This concern needs to include correspondence, word processor screens, etc.

The above list does not imply an unthinking application of all these elements. However, they do each require consideration in relation to the overall purposes of the organization and the client group that it hopes to serve. Decisions might be taken, for example, to use cushions instead of chairs or to invite clients to leave their shoes at the door. What is the case for these decisions and are there any contrary tendencies that will also have to be catered for?

The choice of visual images can also be problematic. How might the images selected contribute to the client's sense of comfort, familiarity and of being respected? Culture-specific images not being related to the culture of the client group may have little impact. For example a poster of an impressionist painting or a framed photograph of people at the Royal Ascot race meeting on Ladies Day may reflect staff values but bear little relation to clients' lives. Images of sacred buildings, historic sites and religious deities will all have impact, as will photographs of people. A certain understanding or sensitivity towards the underlying messages and values transmitted by such images is certainly required in deciding what goes on the walls and why.

Though brief, these proposals are certainly not easy to implement. Nevertheless, a basic survey of clients using a counselling service in the 1970s revealed their discomfort in using an agency that had no culturally relevant images to them as a group.

People matters

> Discriminatory practices result from ways in which the services are organised – selection procedures, points of comparison for promotion etc. (in the case of staff) and diagnostic processes, selective criteria for types of treatment, indicators of dangerousness etc. (in the case of patients). Racism may have direct advantage for the dominant white population in that, for example, the exclusion of black staff from management, and the easing out of black patients from time consuming types of 'sophisticated' treatment modalities or their labelling as (psychiatrically) dangerous allows white society to continue its dominance.
>
> (Fernando 1988)

In Chapter 2 a short organizational case study was given in which the complex issues of inequality were raised within the structure of a counselling agency. Using that case study as a basis, the following sections depict some of the key issues that will require attention in any agency where transcultural therapy is to be offered.

Management structures

How is the agency to be managed? There are many varieties of management practice that range from voluntary committees on the one hand to named, salaried heads or directors on the other. In between, various combinations of these practices might also involve the consultation of and management by staff groups and user groups.

Several important questions relating to the essential work of the agency underpin the above structures:

- Who is involved?
- What is/are their function/s?
- What power do they have?
- Where does the formal decision-making lie?
- Where does the informal decision-making lie?

Establishment of policy

Inevitably, there is often a very strong relationship between the establishment of policy and the management structure of an organization. Policy may both precede practice and/or be generated and modified by practice. Central to these processes must be a concern for the optimum delivery of the therapeutic endeavour to the community it is designed to serve. Attention, therefore, needs to be focused on the involvement of this community within the policy-setting functions and reviews of service delivery.

An organization will inevitably reflect the culture in which it is embedded and the cultural mores held by organizational members. Where organizations may be composed of members originating from differing cultural backgrounds and (in the case of counselling) where the counsellors may have been schooled in different systems of theory, there is likely to be the development of a very complex organizational subculture.

Consultation with the client community while taking into account the organization's decision-making machinery and the effects of group dynamics upon everyone involved are all factors contributing to the complexity of the establishment of policy and good practice. A further dimension of this already challenging scenario is that of the funding sources of the agency and the extent to which its activities are determined by the providers of financial resources.

The counselling team

How are they selected? By what criteria? Who are they? What span of age range, race, culture, gender and faith do they represent? How are they trained? Is the training in-house, external, full-time, part-time, compulsory, short-term, long-term, theoretically homogeneous or diverse, etc.?

Such a huge range of questions appears daunting. Nevertheless the patterns of selection and training will influence therapeutic outcomes for clients who use the agency. Within these two dimensions of selection and training also lie decisions about the employment and involvement of, or liaison with, other forms of helpers, e.g. traditional healers, religious elders, etc. In short, how might the counselling agency extend its capacity to respond sensitively and therapeutically to the client demands placed upon it?

Monitoring outcomes of therapy

The training that most counsellors will have received – a point made elsewhere in this book – will have been derived from Eurocentric models of therapy. Larson (1982) argues that traditionally trained counsellors tend to believe they are competent enough to adapt to any differences among clients and serve their best interests. However, several authors have challenged this false assumption of believed efficacy by researching client experiences of therapy (Thomas and Sillen 1972; Ridley 1995). Consequently an important and often neglected professional activity within most counselling agencies is that of monitoring counsellor effectiveness and client satisfaction. Both numerical and qualitative analysis of client usage of the service will provide the counselling organization with valuable data as to future policy, practice and further training.

This 'feedback loop' of client experience into the organizational process is desirable in all therapeutic situations but in the delivery of transcultural therapy we would argue that it is vital. The very complexity of transcultural therapy demands that counsellor assumptions of helpfulness are not a sufficient basis upon which to establish future practice.

Concluding thoughts

The quote by Hofstede at the beginning of this chapter points us to the dynamic maelstrom of tendencies that support and reinforce a culture's beliefs and practices. This chapter has attempted an examination of the context of a counselling organization, thus provoking the central questions of its suitability to the culturally different clients who use the service. All methods of assessing the efficacy and sensitivity of the counselling practice in relation to cultural difference have to be valued and noted.

This raises many difficulties and challenges to the organization and the various people within it. To be open to constant challenge and to attempt modifications to procedures and practice may become an enormous source of stress for the practitioners. Nevertheless this pales into insignificance when compared with the stresses imposed upon culturally and racially different clients by uninformed, insensitive and inappropriate methods of therapy.

The organization (and the therapists within it) concerned to offer a transcultural service must have clear aims and high commitment to the groups of people they wish to serve, accompanied by professional reflectiveness and integrity.

—*10*———————————

Supervision and consultancy: supporting the needs of therapists in multicultural and multiracial settings

> Counselling Supervision is still in its infancy in any structural form in
> Britain today. Training courses are emerging but are still few, nationally
> . . . and there is no requirement for counsellors to be trained as supervisors
> before undertaking the role of supervisor to other counsellors.
>
> (Thompson 1991, Introduction)

Introduction

The above quote is taken from the introduction to Joyce Thompson's
research into the manner in which the issues of race and culture are dealt with
on training courses in supervision. Her findings, discussed later in the
chapter, reveal these courses' general lack of attention to the issues but an
accompanying enthusiasm for their inclusion on future courses.

A clear consensus exists in the United States literature that clinical
supervision is one of the most important ingredients in the training of
psychotherapists. This consensus prevails across various psychotherapeutic
disciplines such as social work, psychology and psychiatry (Loganbill et al.
1982).

Ivey (1982) used supervision as a variable within the microcounselling
approach in teaching basic counselling skills to masters degree students in
counselling and guidance. Under experimental conditions it was determined
that students who worked with a supervisor in their group performed
significantly better than those who did not.

Despite an increasing number of books and articles about supervision, the
empirical research on it is rather circumscribed. Most of the research is
restricted to the truncated range of psychotherapists' experience in the
examination of trainees rather than advanced psychotherapists (Holloway
and Hosford 1983).

Earlier literature and research in the United States revealed that:

- Supervision was one of the top five activities psychologists engaged in (Garfield and Kurtz 1976).
- More than two thirds of counselling psychologists provided clinical supervision (Fitzgerald and Osipow quoted in Thompson 1991: 3)
- Less than 10 to 15 per cent of supervisors had trained in supervision (Hess 1982).
- Little was known about how supervisors assume the supervisory role; and the full extent of supervisors' responsibilities and legal liabilities were not necessarily evident to supervisees or supervisors (Loganbill et al. 1982).

In addition, McCarthy et al. (1988) asserted that there is no standard literature or solid theoretical base of syllabus for supervision. Carroll (1988) also noted that supervision was still tied to counselling theory despite its efforts to become a discipline of its own, yet he believed strongly that it was on the verge of a professional breakthrough in Britain. This is shown in the development by the British Association for Counselling of its *Code of Ethics and Practice for the Supervision of Counsellors* (British Association of Counselling 1987) and its creation of a scheme for the recognition of supervisors.

However, the available literature in Britain in the 1980s did not emphasize the need for formal training in supervision or the examination of variables such as race and culture in the therapeutic relationship (Carroll 1988; Hawkins and Shohet 1989; Proctor 1989; Dryden and Thorne 1991). Nevertheless Shohet and Wilmot (in Dryden and Thorne 1991: 88) do note that race, along with age, sex, ideology, boundaries, power, control and confidentiality could all be issues that block the progress of the supervisor/supervisee relationship.

What is supervision?

The BAC *Code of Ethics and Practice for the Supervision of Counsellors* (British Association for Counselling 1987) states that 'The primary purpose of supervision is to ensure that the counsellor is addressing the needs of the client.'

The following definition of supervision is taken from the *Dictionary of Counselling* (Feltham and Dryden 1993: 186):

Supervision, literally the overseeing of counsellor's work, supervision protects the client and supports the counsellor. Regarded as a professional and ethical necessity for practising counsellors, supervision takes various forms but all address key elements of a counsellor's work; its professional and ethical boundaries; the competence and continuing professional and personal development of counsellors; the skilful and

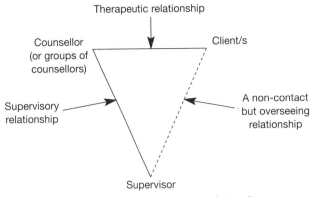

Figure 10.1   The triangular supervision relationship

purposeful use of therapeutic techniques; client material and client–counsellor interaction; the well-being of counsellors themselves. Counselling itself being an emergent profession, supervision is a relatively recent discipline within counselling. Models of supervision differ according to the orientations of counsellor and supervisor . . .

Forms of supervision may include one-to-one, peer and group situations. A relationship that can be conceptualized as triangular is created when supervision is undertaken by the therapist to enhance their work with their client as shown in Figure 10.1. This diagram depicts the therapeutic relationship that exists between the counsellor and client and the supervisory relationship between counsellor and supervisor. The broken line between supervisor and client is indicative of the purpose of supervision, namely that through the supervisory relationship with the counsellor, the supervisor ensures that the needs of the client are addressed sensitively and ethically.

This whole book is geared towards the exploration of the complex issues that exist when counsellor and client hail from different racial and cultural origins. With the addition of a supervisory component to the therapist's work in transcultural counselling comes a new range of complex challenges. Writers have observed that disregarding the influence of cultural factors on the supervisory relationship can contribute to considerable conflict in the supervision process (Guitterez 1982; Cook 1983). Earlier findings by Vandervolk (1974) in the USA revealed that prior to any supervision, black supervisees anticipated less supervisor empathy, respect and congruence than white supervisees. With such apprehension being experienced by black supervisees it would be reassuring to report that white supervisors' attitudes were positively orientated towards black supervisees. However, Helms (1982) found that a predominantly white sample of supervisors perceived that supervisees 'of colour' (a term widely used in the USA and meant to include Asian, black and Hispanic people) were less able to accept

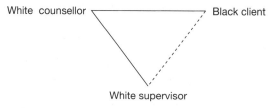

Figure 10.2   The racial complexity of the triangular supervisory relationship (I)

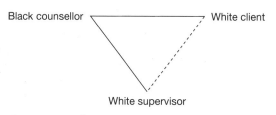

Figure 10.3   The racial complexity of the triangular supervisory relationship (II)

constructive criticism, less open to self-examination and as having more problems keeping appointments than white supervisees. In contrast to white supervisees' self-evaluations, supervisees of colour evaluated themselves more positively on these dimensions than their supervisors did.

In reporting the above findings, Thompson, in her dissertation, goes on to say that:

> it seems therefore that Helms's findings indicate that cross-culturally/ cross-racially mixed dyads are more conflictual than racially homogeneous dyads and that supervisors may also contribute to this conflict. If either speculation is true then we may expect visible racial/cultural group supervisees to experience considerable discomfort or dissatisfaction with cross-cultural/ cross-racial supervision.
>
> (Thompson 1991: 5)

The triangular supervisory relationship

We have already alluded to triangular supervisory relationships that have differing transcultural dimensions. For example, just using the simpler descriptive terms of black and white this triangular relationship can look like Figures 10.2 and 10.3.

In Figure 10.2 the transcultural element is embodied in the counsellor/client dyad, and in Figure 10.3, the counsellor/supervisor relationship. Thompson conceptualized a further six different combinations of this triangular relationship in her dissertation (see Figure 10.4 for all eight).

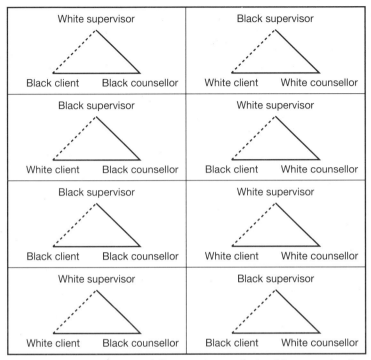

Figure 10.4   Complexities of the supervisory relationship: a matrix of possible triads

Much has already been said in previous chapters about the many levels of potential misunderstanding, the effects of prejudice and stereotyping, the impact of language and so on that may occur within the transcultural relationship. Each and every one of these phenomena apply as equally to the supervisory relationship as they do to the therapeutic relationship. The white supervisor working with a white counsellor who is discussing their work with a black client may have not begun to think about or indeed raised their own awareness of the implications surrounding transcultural counselling. Their method of responding to the counsellor's concerns will be informed by their normal theoretical perspective and consequently will not take into account any data that pertains to the client's cultural and racial self.

Similarly the white supervisor with a black counsellor already has a transculturally supervisory relationship potentially beset with difficulty as described by Thompson above.

At the present time it is likely that the majority of supervisors are likely to be white, a factor that generally impoverishes the potential for more extensive development of therapists in the field and consequently may affect the levels of sensitivity, skill and knowledge counsellors are able to bring to their work with clients.

Supervisors, when consulted by counsellors from different racial or cultural origins to their own or when consulted about clients who are culturally or racially different, will be under pressure to attempt to understand the presented dynamics and story. If untrained and/or insensitive to this arena all they have to offer is the 'same as usual' responses geared to their present understanding. It is likely that they will be keen to be seen to be of professional use to the counsellor and this pressure may well lead them to present themselves as more knowledgeable, more aware and more informed than they really are on these issues.

Likewise, the less secure and/or perhaps trainee counsellor will be keen to impress the supervisor and similarly put on a front of 'knowingness' and competence.

This overall scenario now looks like a not too honourable or honest relationship in which both participants are engaged in impressing one another sufficiently in order to retain both self-esteem and esteem in the face of the other. These collusive dynamics are extremely subtle and at best might eventually contribute towards the creation of a more trusting secure relationship between counsellor and supervisor where real differences and ignorances might be honestly shared. Unfortunately, the same dynamics might be perpetuated and thus become corrosive, dishonest and ultimately of little benefit to the counsellor and certainly not protective enough of the needs of the culturally or racially different client.

The demands on supervisors, professionally and educationally

The factor of the disproportionately high number of white supervisors – which in part, reflects the smaller numbers of black people first of all entering counselling training and then fewer going on to become supervisors – makes it professionally incumbent upon supervisors to develop their own skills in this specific arena. Atkinson et al. (1985) suggested that supervisors need to have some general knowledge about the racial/cultural identity process, information about cultural norms and conflicts between black and whites, and also a willingness to address how trainees/counsellors manage their anxiety in situations where differences are present (see also Atkinson 1985).

Hunt (1986) suggests that a culturally sensitive supervisor understands the differences in transcultural counselling and can help trainees learn facilitative behaviours in transcultural interactions.

Notwithstanding the above assertions, it seems reasonable to assume that many supervisors, who themselves may have trained as therapists quite a few years ago, will not have been exposed to these issues within their own training or indeed in their clinical practice with clients and will, therefore, not be sufficiently sensitive or informed about them in the supervisory process.

All of the above leads us to conclude that specialist training of supervisors in these areas is of utmost urgency. Supervisors have potentially an enormous impact upon counsellors and their practice. The significance of their role can be equated to that of their trainers in the creation of sound professional and ethical practice.

In supervisor training Thompson suggests the following issues as worthy of exploration:

- power in the counselling/supervisory relationship
- perceived power and colonial history and its implications for effective practice
- countertransference issues between counsellor and client and between counsellor and supervisor
- parallel process issues between supervisor and supervisee
- the danger of collusion and over-identification with counsellors and between counsellors and clients
- the importance of role models and positive images
- the facts and mechanisms of racism and the effects of oppression
- black people's expectations of white people
- white people's expectations of black people
- black/white people's perceptions and expectations of other black/white people in differing roles
- advantages and disadvantages of working in same race triads (counsellor, client, supervisor).

All of the above will also require contextualizing within the supervisor's own theoretical model. Again, the implications of this sentence are very considerable indeed despite its few words!

As mentioned earlier, the development of theoretical models of supervision is still in its early stages. Many supervisors inevitably employ their theoretical models of therapy within the supervisory process. Similar to the challenge facing transcultural therapists, supervisors also have to consider carefully how the many dimensions of difference (of cultural, racial and linguistic difference, power differences of racial identity, etc.) all described elsewhere in this book can be incorporated, in an informal way, into their professional task of supervision.

Let us return to the statement of purpose taken from the BAC *Code of Ethics and Practice for the Supervision of Counsellors* (British Association for Counselling 1987): 'The primary purpose of supervision is to ensure that the counsellor is addressing the needs of the client.' The implications of this statement are far reaching indeed.

The supervisor might be working with a counsellor who is relatively unaware of these issues yet who has one or several clients who are culturally and racially different. If the supervisor seeks to fulfil their professional commitment in such circumstances their task is formidable. They will have to employ some of the following methods and strategies to support and educate the counsellor: teaching, information provision, knowledge of relevant texts, ideas about relevant referral resources, a fund of pertinent metaphors and stories, a desire to pursue joint learning with the supervisee, a wish to go beyond their own cultural and theoretical boundaries, a willingness to consult further expertise and so on.

The above methods imply that the supervisor of transcultural therapists must have sufficient personal knowledge and preferably personal experience acquired through personal, clinical and training experiences to meet these very high professional demands.

The timely relevance and pertinence of Thompson's research is clear: the supervisor of transcultural therapists needs to be extremely knowledgeable, clinically very experienced and open to much new learning if they are to measure up to the important task assigned them within transcultural therapy.

—11—

Training therapists to work with different client groups

A body of literature exists that documents the widespread ineffectiveness of traditional counselling approaches and techniques when applied to racial and ethnic minority populations . . . it is apparent that the major reason for therapeutic ineffectiveness lies in the training of mental health professionals.

(Sue et al. 1992: 478)

Introduction

Many basic counselling training courses within the United Kingdom, for example, spend relatively little time and attention on the preparation of counselling trainees to work with culturally and racially different clients. Given the huge amount of material to be learned in terms of knowledge acquisition and skill development in counselling and psychotherapy this situation is understandable, though it becomes less defensible within the reality of the UK as a multiracial society.

At a theoretical level there is an important debate as to when specialist training in transcultural therapy should take place. By contrast with the United States and Canada, where it is possible to do graduate and postgraduate degrees in this subject, the majority of therapist training in the UK is part-time, attracts students who are often mature and already professionally qualified (within other disciplines) and is frequently geared to a monotheoretical view (i.e. a training in psychodynamic or person-centred or gestalt approaches, etc.). These issues of training are clearly related to the relatively short history of the activity/profession within Britain, the reality that many counsellors are part-time or voluntary, and the fact that there is not an easily identifiable or coherent professional structure of careers within counselling and psychotherapy.

In the training of transcultural therapists a primary debate has to be the consideration of whether this training can be done effectively at initial qualification level or on post-qualification courses. The argument of high-volume input on initial courses has to be balanced with that of considering students who may be highly motivated to work in transcultural therapy but who cannot afford or are not traditionally qualified to pursue higher courses.

Certainly Boyd-Franklin (1989) and Lee and Richardson (1991) value the importance of ongoing professional training and development opportunities after initial training. Initial counsellor training, however, must begin to help students address some of the basic issues, thus encouraging a sensitivity to the whole subject (Boyd-Franklin 1989). Specialist courses in the UK on this subject are still few and far between and tend more towards short workshop programmes rather than being longer qualification-based academic courses. The selection of students is always a difficult task for trainers. Selection based purely on culture or race will be too simplistic, and would not recognize that shared cultural background does not guarantee a successful therapeutic relationship (D'Ardenne and Mahtani 1989; Moodley 1991).

Training partners and teams that comprise colleagues who themselves are culturally and racially different have become accepted in practice as epitomizing useful role models and representing the complexity of data that needs to be addressed within the training.

Students and trainees: selection and motivation

Change is water flowing under bridges,
Change is boundaries dissolved,
Change is being lost in strange readiness to end or to begin,
Change is challenge to begin ever anew.
Change is freedom, hardly won to live a new and unpredicted life new shaped.

(Clark 1982: 303)

There is no doubt that exposure to the ideas, theories, attitudes and skills that underpin this subject can have disturbing implications for the trainees. McLeod (1993: 110) acknowledges that counsellors exhibit a general avoidance of political issues and few attempts have been made to develop a theoretical understanding of the issues involved in counselling people from different social classes (Pilgrim 1992).

For those students who enrol on longer specialist courses on transcultural therapy a generalized commitment to helping others may not be sufficient motivation to see them through the enormous challenges they will have to face with regards to their own concepts of the world and how it operates. Training in this arena has the potential to go to the core of one's own cultural and racial identity and present demanding questions and disturbing scenarios. In cases of student selection, courses might have to decide upon what criteria trainees are chosen and one of those criteria might usefully be related to the psychology of 'heroic helpers' as defined by Staub (1993). Certainly it is the authors' experience that such courses implicitly invite participants to take a position in relation to race relations, immigration matters, issues of power in society and so on. Exposure to the training issues inevitably invites personal introspection at a very deep level. High student motivation will certainly be required.

An openness to consider other theoretical and cultural approaches to counselling and helping is certainly advocated by a variety of writers (Lago and Thompson 1989a; Lee and Richardson 1991; Sue et al. 1992). This factor may be hard pressed by students who have attended previous monotheoretically based courses. Trainees and their trainers also need to commit themselves to the question of how they might adapt theories and techniques of traditional counselling approaches to meet different cultural needs.

The training task: empowerment and enablement

Nancy Boyd-Franklin (1989) makes a strong case for the empowerment of therapists through training in order that they may also empower their clients. Indeed the concept of client empowerment has always been an aim of counselling in general and advocated as being central to any work with refugees (Stringer 1992). Nevertheless, there are substantial contradictions beneath the ideology of empowerment. In short, empowerment cannot be assumed to be a natural outcome of therapy (McLeod 1993).

Troyna (1994) was so concerned about the 'blind faith' assertions of educational researchers in relation to the empowering effects of their research that he wrote a paper advocating caution and more attention to clarity of intent and definition. He cites the work of Jennifer Gore (1993), who argues that empowerment

> carries with it an agent of empowerment (someone or something doing the empowering), a notion of power as property (to *em*-power implies to give or confer power) and a vision or desired end state (some vision of what it is to be empowered and the possibility of a state of empowerment).
>
> (pp. 73–4)

Troyna cites other researchers who have usefully drawn a distinction between empowerment and 'giving a voice' (Ellsworth 1989; Gurnah 1992). The two concepts are often used interchangeably but may have quite contradictory outcomes, he argues.

These issues pose a considerable challenge to trainers and to therapists to consider carefully their claims, their intentions and the possible outcomes of therapy. Notwithstanding, it is clear that Boyd-Franklin (1989) is concerned

Table 11.1 Key recommendations for multiculturally skilled counsellors characteristics

Dimensions	Counsellor awareness of own assumptions, values and biases	Understanding the world view of the culturally different client	Developing appropriate intervention strategies and techniques
Beliefs and attitudes	Culturally skilled counsellors: • are aware and sensitive to own cultural heritage and to valuing and respecting differences • are aware of how their own cultural background influences psychological processes • are able to recognize their limits • are comfortable with differences between them and clients.	Culturally skilled counsellors: • are aware of their emotional reactions towards other racial and ethnic groups • are aware of their stereotypes and preconceived notions.	Culturally skilled counsellors: • respect clients' spiritual beliefs and values • respect indigenous helping practices • value bilingualism.
Knowledge	Culturally skilled counsellors: • have knowledge about their racial/cultural heritage and how it affects definitions of normality and process of counselling • possess knowledge and understanding about the workings of oppression/racism/discrimination (refers to white identity development model) • possess knowledge about their social impact upon others.	Culturally skilled counsellors: • possess specific knowledge and information about the particular group they are working with (refers to the minority identity development model) • understand how race/culture/ethnicity may affect personality formation/vocational choice/psychological disorder/help-seeking behaviour • understand and have knowledge of socio-political influences that impinge upon racial/ethnic minorities.	Culturally skilled counsellors: • have clear knowledge of limits of counselling and how they may clash with minority values • are aware of institutional barriers preventing minorities' access to mental health services • understand limits of assessment procedures • have knowledge of minority family structures and community hierarchy.
Skills	Culturally skilled counsellors: • seek out educational consultative and training experiences to enrich their understanding • constantly seek to understand themselves as racial/cultural beings and actively seek a non-racist identity.	Culturally skilled counsellors: • should familiarize themselves with relevant research regarding various groups and seek out educational opportunities that enrich their knowledge, understanding and skills • become involved with minority individuals outside the counselling setting so that their perspective is wider-informed.	Culturally skilled counsellors: • have a broad range of help-styles • are able to exercise institutional intervention skills • are willing to consult a wide range of other helpers • take responsibility for interest in language required by the client.

Source: Based on Sue et al. 1992.

to explore how trainee therapists might be enabled to mobilize all their potential for working skilfully and sensitively in transcultural therapeutic settings.

Lago, H. (1994) cites management consultants Byham and Cox (1988), who define four areas of activity that are required for 'empowerment' to work:

• direction (key result areas, goals, measurements)
• knowledge (skills, training, information, goals)
• resources (tools, materials, facilities, money)
• support (approval, coaching, feedback, encouragement).

Converting the above concepts from a managerial into an educational context, we would assert that:

• direction equates to the goals of the training
• knowledge can be subdivided into beliefs and attitudes, knowledge and skills
• resources are those required for the training (including clinical placements) and
• support relates to the work of tutors, fellow students and supervisors on the course.

Multicultural counselling competencies

Sue et al. (1992) published a set of multicultural counselling competencies in the USA that have been reproduced in an abbreviated form as Table 11.1. (The abbreviations on the matrix are ours and we apologize for any inaccuracies conveyed by our condensation of the original.) Conceived originally as a basis for outlining the need and rationale for a multicultural perspective in counselling, the Professional Standards Committee of the (American) Association for Multicultural Counselling and Development went much further in proposing 31 multicultural counselling competencies and urging the counselling profession in the United States to adopt these as accreditation criteria. Two of the leading journals cooperated on publishing the same article in both their editions as a service to the profession.

The matrix developed by Sue et al. (1992) is derived from earlier attempts to identify specific crosscultural counselling competencies that have traditionally been divided into three dimensions: beliefs and attitudes; knowledge; and skills. These three dimensions are set against the three characteristics of: counsellor awareness of own assumptions, values and biases; understanding the world views of the culturally different client; and developing appropriate intervention strategies and techniques.

For reasons of clarity of presentation, the following sections that depict the aims of training follow the above example by being divided into the three major areas of beliefs, knowledge and skill.

Beliefs, attitudes and awareness

In addition to Sue et al. (1992), Webb Johnson (1993), D'Ardenne and Mahtani (1989) and Lago and Thompson (1989a) have all previously made recommendations concerning training and counselling practice within transcultural therapy. Not surprisingly, there is considerable agreement across these sources about the major elements required in any transcultural therapy training.

This first section thus concentrates upon the importance of the counsellor's own sense of who they are culturally and racially and what this means in terms of their beliefs, attitudes and behaviours. This awareness comes from developing their understanding and appreciation of the cultural context within which they have been raised and now live. A recent article by Phoenix (1994) gives a clue as to the difficulty such an endeavour creates when one considers the multiple subject-positions we all occupy, which change over time and situation. Ponterotto and Pedersen (1993) offer an extensive overview of the current theories of identity development in the United States. These models may contribute significantly to the trainee's own understanding of where they position themselves within society.

Training exercises that facilitate this exploration of roots and origins require handling with great sensitivity because of the personal material they might provoke in students. This personal work is really never fully completed and certainly cannot be achieved in an afternoon's training session! It is important that trainers inculcate a view of this personal work as an ongoing element of professional development for therapists.

From such work it is hoped that trainees will gain an awareness of both their own and others' deep cultural, racial and spiritual frameworks of being, thinking and living. This awareness will also enhance their understanding of their own stereotypes, assumptions and judgements, and help them to appreciate the very different psychological and cultural frameworks by which other people live. It will also inform their own processes of self-monitoring in relation to negative attitudes they may have whilst conducting transcultural interviews and help them avoid imposing their own frame of reference upon clients.

Skilled tutoring and competent clinical supervision will also assist trainees to appreciate the more subtle and complex areas of this personal dimension and foster understanding of the myriad ways in which unconscious imposition of values can be powerfully transmitted from therapist to clients in ways that are neither useful or therapeutic.

Rogers asserts, within his person-centred theory that 'the organism [person] acts as an organised whole to their phenomenal field' (Rogers 1987: 486). The pursuit of awareness being advocated here will hopefully reveal the truth of the above statement and lead the students to respect the organized wholeness of the culturally different client, a phenomenon quite opposed to the invisibility that many ethnic minority clients experience in this society (Phung 1995).

Knowledge

This characteristic, like the ones in the preceding and succeeding sections, provides a considerable challenge to the learner, the teacher and the process they are engaged upon. The concept of knowledge, as described here, is of the quality that becomes internalized within the student, not a unit of external facts to be assembled for an examination and then forgotten. The focus here is on how the knowledge informs and illuminates therapist practice.

Sue et al. (1992) have considerably developed and expanded this dimension beyond the sets of suggestions made by the British writers, d'Ardenne and Mahtani (1989), Lago and Thompson (1989a), Webb-Johnson (1993) and Phung (1995). This, perhaps, is to be expected as it reflects a set of concerns and research efforts that have been pursued by the therapy professions for much longer in the United States.

To become a transculturally skilled counsellor, students will need to:

- have knowledge about the complex concepts of race, culture, ethnicity and how these relate to their own heritage and thus affect their perceptions of the world
- gain understanding of the historical and contemporary relations between their own culture and others
- understand how systems of racism and oppression operate
- attain specific knowledge about the client group/s they may work with, including family systems and community hierarchies
- understand how race, culture and ethnicity impacts upon people's development and informs and motivates their actions in society
- understand how the processes of the dominant group in society impacts upon minority group members
- consider the impact of language difference from clients and construct strategies to deal with this
- have knowledge of the cultural limits of counselling.

All these points are geared towards ensuring that therapists do not misuse their power (personal, gender-related, cultural, racial, institutional) with clients and that they also do not impose culturally biased views or procedures for action that will effectively be harmful to clients.

Skills

> In sum, skills training should centre around how to incorporate the cultural dynamics and naturally occurring support systems of diverse groups of people into counselling interventions.
>
> (Lee and Richardson 1991: 210)

An underlying yet core concept within this dimension of skills acquisition is that of becoming and of being perceived as a competent communicator. Rogers (1959) has always stressed that it is not good enough for the therapist to be skilled but that the client has to perceive that the therapist's skills, intentions and commitment are present. Gudykunst (1994) has very usefully described several major themes that underline competent communications skills in crosscultural encounters. These include the abilities to be mindful, tolerate ambiguity, be able to manage anxiety, be able to adapt and to empathize. Indeed he asserts that the one skill that most consistently emerges in discussions of effective communication with 'strangers' is that of empathy (p. 184).

An interesting pan-historical review of the evolution of human consciousness by Neville (1994) suggests that human beings have a wide range of capacity for empathic understanding of their fellows. This spans from preverbal sensing through to a fourth-dimension perception which he suggests is part of a new, emerging evolutionary phase of human consciousness in the latter part of this century.

However, Jones (1987) urges caution in the unthinking transfer of empathic inference, where one's own feelings and thoughts are used as an index of what another is experiencing. This technique is traditionally based upon a bond of similarity of individuals. Crosscultural psychotherapy is necessarily problematic, since empathy defined in terms of understanding others on the basis of shared qualities cannot occur. There is a need for an empathy based on differences, he argues, which focuses the imagination upon transposing itself into another, rather than upon one's own feelings; and in this way, psychotherapists might achieve a more complete understanding of culturally varied predispositions, personal constructs and experience (p. 178).

D'Ardenne and Mahtani (1989: 39) provide an excellent list of 17 skills deemed appropriate for transcultural therapists, which span the realm of direct skills (listening, linguistic competence, non-verbal, interpretation of expression, organizational, etc.) to commitment to development (of self, of knowledge, of language acquisition, etc.).

The capacity of counsellors to respond with a range of therapeutic interventions is one that is widely accepted within the North American literature on this subject (see Table 11.1). Our present understanding is that a much broader range of psychotherapeutic approaches are introduced on counsellor training programmes in the United States and Canada as compared to the UK. Many British courses tend towards the dissemination of perhaps one particular approach, with the other approaches being addressed only in a subsidiary manner.

Given this broad educational context of counselling training in North America, the acquisition of a wide range of therapeutic intervention skills may not be so problematic as it might prove in Britain, where trainers and supervisors may demonstrate some considerable resistance to approaches other than their own. For example, research outcomes of behaviour therapy in the USA clearly show the effectiveness of such approaches in the treatment of clients from any race or ethnic background (Kolko 1987; Paniagua 1994). Various authors argue that this is because these strategies are authoritative, concrete, action-orientated and emphasize immediate, focused learning factors preferred by certain specific cultural groups (Walker and La Due 1986; Boyd-Franklin 1989; Paniagua 1994).

Despite this evidence, we believe that ideological differences between adherents of different theoretical persuasions in Britain might prove stumbling blocks to the development of multiply skilled counsellor training. This debate does give insight into the cultural, theoretical and professional differences between North America and Britain. Certainly a range of writings in Britain suggest the successful use of a range of theories with culturally different clients (e.g. Mahtani 1989; Kareem and Littlewood 1992; Lago 1992; Eleftheriadou 1994; McDevitt 1994). This availability of different schools of therapists in Britain may be compared to the range of healers in Brazil described in Chapter 7. The difference may occur, however, in the levels of client understanding of what these differences might mean in practice. Because of the relatively short history of counselling in Britain, it is likely that differences between counselling approaches will not be appreciated by most clients. Perhaps the beginning of a resolution to the above seeming differences may be found in a statement in Webb Johnson's article (1993: 26): 'Different schools of counselling are not as significant as the attitudes and skills of the individual therapist.'

Skills for organizational and development work

The general activity of working as a therapist inevitably involves some organizational skills. Therapists often work in organizations and as such, require good communication and liaison skills. In addition they need to be able to establish good working relationships with referring organizations. These dimensions obviously apply to most therapeutic settings.

Koslow and Salett (1989: 150) argue strongly that transcultural therapists need to be able to: work within the realities and needs of the organization, function effectively within that organization and also manage the counselling process in organizational settings. This aspect of skills acquisition will hopefully be addressed in the therapist's training course and as a result of supervised experience on the counselling placement.

In our previous writing on the subject (Lago and Thompson 1989a) we suggested that counsellors who engage in transcultural counselling may inevitably become involved in training and preventive, educational work within the fields of crosscultural relations, anti-racism and so on. The processes of training outlined above and then subsequent clinical transcultural practice will equip and furnish each therapist with extensive knowledge and unique insight for later use in the training domain.

All training courses are limited in the extent to which they may contribute to student development; this may be something that only each individual can nurture some time after their training course.

Where, how and with what?

This section addresses, in outline form, the issues of educational approaches and resources that will have to be considered by trainers planning transcultural therapy courses. Many of these aspects will be familiar to trainers already, though the specific demands of the transcultural element may mean a search for new developments in approach and new locations for clinical practice. (A valuable résumé of intercultural criteria for mental health training may be found in Pedersen 1985.)

Where? (is the training conducted?)

- in the classroom
- in clinical placements
- in supervision (with a culturally different supervisor?)
- on visits
- in personal therapy (with a culturally different therapist?)
- in training groups and community meetings (see Mearns 1994 for a further explanation of the value of community meetings on training courses).

How?

- lectures
- seminars (student presented)
- group discussion
- multicultural/multiracial communication groups
- workshops
- experiential approaches
- simulated therapeutic interviews/role play/possible audio or televisually recorded for later analysis
- direct therapeutic practice
- diary keeping
- research activities
- reading the literature
- preparing written assignments
- case study discussion.

With what?

Trainers may be hard-pressed in locating ideas and resources for conducting experiential sessions. Certainly there exists a lot of room for new developments in this arena. A few suggestions for ideas are listed in the appendix to this chapter, which if pursued, will lead readers to further resources and references.

Summing up

We are aware of how much material has not been included within the text. The authors' own experiences of running short courses on this subject reveal the extent to which the subject-matter has the potential both to inform as well as to upset profoundly participants' views of themselves and others. This was hinted at in the early sections on student motivation and selection. The prospect of stimulating and enabling students to acquire the necessary awareness, knowledge and skills is a daunting one for trainers, especially when one bears in mind the short-life and part-time nature of most transcultural counselling courses. This reductionist tendency may be further exacerbated by the poverty of resources available to training courses by way of appropriate teaching and learning facilities, and purchase of training media. Some specialist courses are now, inevitably, rather costly and consequently disadvantage some admirable and talented applicants from poorer backgrounds.

Despite this rather bleak overview, we wish to encourage training organizations to embrace this important dimension of transcultural therapy training. However short the courses are, even one-day workshops, potential exists for sowing the seeds of interest and commitment; any multicultural/ multiracial society deserves skilled transcultural therapists.

Appendix to Chapter 11: a brief list of training resources

Culture and cultural identity

Baker, K.G. (1989) A workshop model for exploring ones' cultural identity, in D.R. Koslow and E.P Salett (eds) *Crossing Cultures in Mental Health*. Washington DC: SIETAR.

Casse, P. (1981) *Training for the Cross Cultural Mind*. Washington, DC: SIETAR.

Lago, C.O. (1990) *Working with Overseas Students: A Staff Development Training Manual*. Huddersfield: Huddersfield University and British Council.

Race and anti-racism

Katz, J.H. (1978) *White Awareness: A Handbook for Anti-Racism Training*. Norman, OK: University of Oklahoma Press.

Ponterotto, J.G. and Pedersen, P.B. (1993) *Preventing Prejudice: A Guide for Counsellors and Educators*. Newbury Park, CA: Sage.

Development of cultural/racial identity

Ponterotto, J.G. and Pedersen, P.B. (1993) *Preventing Prejudice: A Guide for Counsellors and Educators*. Newbury Park, CA: Sage.

Cultural differences in communication

Brislin, R.W., Cushner, K., Cherrie, C. and Yong, M. (1986) *Intercultural Interactions: A Practical Guide*. Beverly Hills, CA: Sage.

Gudykunst, W.B. (1994) *Bridging Differences: Effective Intergroup Communication*, 2nd edn. London: Sage.

Questionnaires

Boyd-Franklin, N. (1989) *Black Families in Therapy: A Multisystems Approach*. New York: Guilford Press. (the use of genograms)

Go-Paul-McNicol, S.A. (1993) *Working with West Indian Families*. New York: Guilford Press. (client attitudes)

Koslow, D.R. and Salett, E.P. (1989) *Crossing Cultures in Mental Health*, p. 20. Washington, DC: SIETAR. (on cultural assumptions)

Koslow and Salett (1989: 151) (organizational settings)

McGrath, P. and Axelson, J.A. (1993) *Accessing Awareness and Developing Knowledge: Foundations for Skills in a Multicultural Society*. Monterey, CA: Brooks/Cole. (values clarification: what do you believe about the human experience?)

Paniagua, F.A. (1994) *Assessing and Treating Culturally Diverse Clients: A Practical Guide*. London: Sage. (exploration of biases)

Training videos

Clark, J. and Lago, C.O. (1981) 'Multi-racial videoscenes'. Leicester: Department of Educational Technology, De Montfort University.

Lago, C.O. and Thompson, J. (1989) 'Issues of race and culture in counselling settings', video and training manual. Leicester: Department of Audio Visual Aids, Leicester University.

Case histories for discussion

Eleftheriadou, Z. (1994) *Transcultural Counselling*. London: Central Books.

Kareem, J. and Littlewood, R. (1992) *Intercultural Therapy: Themes, Interpretations and Practices*. Oxford: Blackwell Scientific.

Training exercises

Pedersen, P.B. (1994) *A Handbook for Developing Multicultural Awareness*. Alexandria, AV: American Counselling Association.

—*12*———————

The challenge of research

> The field of cross-cultural counselling has received relatively little attention
> in the research literature. In addition, many counselling agencies and
> individual counsellors in private practice have so many clients applying
> from their majority cultural group that there is little incentive for them to
> develop expertise in cross-cultural work. The multicultural nature of
> contemporary society, and the existence of large groups of dispossessed
> exiles and refugees experiencing profound hopelessness and loss, make this
> an increasingly important area for future investment in theory, research
> and practice.
>
> (McLeod 1993: 118)

Challenge and complexity

There are two overarching dimensions to this chapter on research. The first is
concerned with the theme of the complexity of the task, and the second
encompasses the fact that so much needs to be done.

A wide variety of research projects have been carried out in the United
States and Canada. Very little, to our knowledge, has been completed in
Britain. This point is further confirmed in an article by Jewel (1994) and
underlined by the absence of citations in a handbook of research (Sutton
1987). We have, from time to time, been consulted by counselling students
around Britain wishing to write projects on this subject. Most frequently,
these studies have been based on literature reviews and reflections on
transcultural counselling practice. In some instances the writers have offered
case studies combined with commentary and critique. All of the above efforts
are of value as they contribute to a growing awareness, knowledge and
literature upon the subject. In addition, an increasing number of articles are
being published in the counselling and psychotherapy journals. The assertion
that so much needs to be done still holds true, both generally and most
specifically in Britain.

In responding to the above challenge, the issue of complexity of task then
confronts the potential researcher. Who do you study? What do you
investigate? How do you go about it? Where? How are the results evaluated?
Let us briefly take these questions and address their implications.

Who is studied? This question is central to the whole task and emanates from a need for researchers to achieve a working definition of the transcultural counselling relationship. The culture, race and ethnicity of both counsellor and client will have immense significance, as will, of course, their differences or similarities in religious orientation, class, gender, language, income level, role and so on. The possible number of combinations of counsellor/client dyads is huge and a mechanism for tolerating or managing this variety will constitute a major challenge.

What is investigated? The purpose of the research will also require much consideration. The task might variously be focused on the communication interaction, on the impact of different theoretical styles, upon an exploration of the effects of projection and countertransference, upon perceived levels of counsellor understanding, upon outcome measures for the client and so on.

The implementation of the necessary research procedures will also constitute a great challenge. How, for example, will counsellors and clients be invited and contracted into the research programme? The demands of ethical practice in this regard alone are considerable. The participants might be subjected to a variety of research procedures such as the following: pre- and post-interview questionnaires, subsequent researcher-led interviews and the use of external evaluators to 'rate' the efficacy of therapeutic procedures. All of the above research approaches inevitably introduce further subsets of procedural quandaries for the researcher. Many of these challenges are inevitable and inherent in the more generalized arena of research in counselling and psychotherapy; these have been confronted over several decades now by research practitioners. Research instruments and question-naires have been developed over time and tested for reliability. Ethical guidelines have been established and mechanisms and procedures for evaluating the impact of counselling upon clients have been created.

These procedures, however, may not be applied so easily to the transcul-tural relationship. For example, if diagnostic evaluations are used, do they apply, or can they be interpreted accurately by the client who is culturally different to the investigator who devised the categories? The inappropriate use of questionnaires applied blindly across races has long been of real and very justified concern as to the racist inferences drawn from the results (Szasz 1970, 1971). In addition, the very motives that drive the researcher cannot be ignored, as research is certainly not a 'neutral' activity (Lehmann 1994).

This brief examination of the complexities facing the researcher of transcultural counselling is admirably summed up by Sue (1988): 'Not enough research has been conducted, and published research suffers from methodological and conceptual limitations' (cited in Jewel 1994: 17).

A further dimension deserves notice. The majority of research work on this subject has been conducted in North America. Though it is considered as inadequate (as suggested above), it nevertheless, by virtue of its very existence, dominates and determines theoretical discourse and clinical practice. What is required is a substantial research effort set within the context of British therapeutic practice and British culture. Previous research is obviously profoundly useful but researchers must not be blind to the cultural context within which it was carried out and how that constitutes a different base for interpreting and understanding the outcomes.

Hypotheses for research

Sundberg constructed a very useful set of 15 'proto-hypotheses' that would lead towards research in intercultural counselling (in Pedersen et al. 1981). He deliberately used the term 'proto-hypotheses' as they were far from having operational definitions. He also acknowledged that many of these points would be seen to be similar for any kind of counselling, though they apply particularly within the transcultural counselling dyad. A precis of his main points appears below.

Mutuality of purposes and helping expectations

1 Counsellors require awareness of different cultures' help-seeking behaviours.
2 The more similar the goals envisaged for counselling between counsellor and client, the more effective therapy will be.
3 The more similar both client and counsellor are towards a whole range of relationship values, the more effective therapy will be (e.g. dependency, power, authority, etc.)
4 The more specific the client's concerns are, the more likely they can be helped.

Developing the counsellor's intercultural understanding and communication skills

5 The counsellor needs to know about socialization processes in the client's culture.
6 Counsellor effectiveness will be enhanced by the counsellor's sensitivity to communication and awareness of other cultures' communication styles.
7 Previous background and training in transcultural interactions will enhance counsellor effectiveness.

Developing the client's intercultural attitudes and skills

8 The less familiar the client is with the counselling process the more the counsellor will need to inform the client about it.

Cultural considerations of the client's areas of action

9 Effectiveness will be increased when mutual knowledge exists about the client's previous assumptive framework in relation to the present and future fields of action.

10 Effectiveness is enhanced by understanding the client's relationship to relevant cultures and significant cultural reference group members.

11 Counsellors need to appreciate the processes of adaptation required in moving across cultures.

12 Extended consideration is required of the client's present living situation and, as a consequence of this, possible decisions after counselling.

13 Despite great differences there are some common elements across cultures and clients, e.g. counsellor flexibility of response, client capacity to tolerate anxiety, etc.

14 Culture-specific methods will be more effective with certain groups than others.

15 The counsellor needs to respect the client as an individual with their own competencies and resources.

The above 'proto-hypotheses' are worthy of contemplation. However, they also reflect a historically specific set of conceptualizations defined by the American cultural context of that time. Very scant attention, for example, is given to the effects of race in terms of racism, power inequalities in society, counsellor-projected attitudes, etc. This focus has been adopted in some of the later American research (cited in Jewel 1994) but it been regarded as a matter of greater concern within the British context (Lago and Thompson 1989a).

Jackson and Meadows (1991) advocate three principal aims of research that are directly related to their notion of culture. Their concern is to stimulate a deeper understanding of the underlying conceptual cultural systems which may be utilized to inform counsellor sensitivity and therapeutic interventions. Also they argue 'that research efforts grounded in well conceived cultural frameworks that are culturally specific have the potential for resolving issues of scientific cultural bias' (p. 75).

Much of the literature on multicultural counselling, training and research has been dominated by a suboptimal conceptual system, assert Speight et al. (1991). In their article advocating a redefinition of multicultural counselling, they explain that there have been two major differing tendencies in the literature. Described as 'etic' and 'emic', the first perspective refers to the universal approach in multicultural theory, practice and research. In research the etic approach emphasizes the development of explanatory constructs applicable to all cultures. The etic approach has merit but a problem of 'imposed etics' arises when explanatory constructs in a particular culture are assumed to be universal and are applied to other cultures without establishing crosscultural equivalency. Sue (1981) has specifically criticized 'imposed etics' because they lead to different views of ethnic group members, as either pathological, genetically deficient, culturally deficient or culturally different (cited in Speight et al. 1991).

The 'emic' approach, by contrast, refers to the culturally specific approach which has been prevalent within anthropological literature and attempts to understand different groups in their own terms rather than by contrast to other reference groups. An emic approach to research thus focuses on understanding behaviour and experience from within the cultural context in which it occurs. From a positive perspective this approach can portray the relationship between an individual and their society but there is a contrary tendency to overemphasize the influence of culture upon the individual and thus minimize all other human factors.

Moving on from the question posed by Sue et al. (1982), 'How can a counsellor and client who differ from each other effectively work together?', Speight et al. (1991) develop an optimal theory that is derived from earlier work by Kluckholm and Murray (1953), Cox (1982) and Ibrahim (1985), and that is also described as having its roots in ancient, traditional African culture. Speight and co-authors explain that Kluckholm and Murray (1953) established a basic paradigm when they argued that every person is like all other persons, is only like some other persons and is also like no other person. Thirty years later, Cox (1982) produced a diagram of three intersecting circles in which individual uniqueness, human universality and cultural specificity are representative of the interactive components influencing humans. To understand individuals fully, Ibrahim (1985) asserted that it is necessary to understand the unique and simultaneous influences of these three domains upon individuals' world views in order to achieve counselling effectiveness (Speight et al. 1991).

The ancient roots of optimal theory are traced back to the beginnings of human culture, where differences are fully integrated into a holistic picture of the individual. This influence is also combined with recent contemporary writings taking a transcendental perspective of universality.

From this theoretical perspective Speight et al. (1991) urge that optimal theory research, which is directed towards understanding rather than controlling or predicting, has to grapple with the influences of individual experience and uniqueness, human universal tenets and cultural specificity. They suggest that researchers might use research approaches that involve naturalistic-ethnographic, phenomenological and cybernetic research paradigms to illuminate meaning and subjective experience.

Certainly the above recognition of human complexity allows for the clinical experiences of the authors who have had both successful and less successful experiences of counselling clients from both near and far, culturally and racially speaking. These experiences have led us to consider the interrelationship between culture and personality and to hypothesize that some people in many cultures, because of their personality type, might be more drawn towards insight-producing, dialogue-based helping rather than other forms of assistance. By contrast, clients who are racially and culturally similar to the counsellors did not find the counselling approach as effective as other approaches because of their particular personality. These contrary indications can also exist within cultural milieux that value and reinforce psychotherapeutic interventions or tend towards other helping interventions.

Racial and ethnic identity development

> The majority of race awareness exercises and prejudice prevention programmes are not solidly grounded in accepted theory of interracial interactions. For this reason, many of them have met with only limited success. However, in the past decade research on racial and ethnic identity development has enabled us to bring a new understanding to the nature of prejudice. Racial identity theory serves as a solid foundation for studying the origins, nature and prevention of prejudice.
> (Pontoretto and Pedersen 1993: 37)

Racial and ethnic identity development has been described by one American academic theorist as 'being at the leading edge of thinking on multicultural counselling in the United States at the present time' (Lee 1994).

A range of models of identity development have now been developed within the United States. In short, these are models that attempt to describe a developmental process that human beings may proceed through in their quest to achieve a healthy sense of racial and ethnic identity. Feeling good about who we are enables us to respect and value others. Consequently the counsellors' own sense of racial identity development becomes an important if not determining component in the crosscultural counselling relationship. Two such models are described below.

Helms's white racial consciousness model (1984) suggests five stages of development: contact, disintegration, reintegration, pseudo-independence and autonomy.

The contact stage is characterized by an unawareness of self as a racial being, a tendency to ignore differences, an awareness that minorities exist yet searches for resolution through withdrawal.

Disintegration involves becoming aware of racism which leads to guilt, depression and negative feelings. There exists a sense of being caught between internal standards of human decency and external cultural expectations. Responses to this dilemma lead to over-identification with black people, the development of paternalistic attitudes towards them or a retreat into white culture.

Reintegration is typified by hostility towards minorities and positive bias in favour of own racial group.

Stage four, the pseudo-independent stage, is marked by an increasing interest in racial group similarities and differences accompanied by an intellectual acceptance of other groups. Limited crossracial interactions or relationships with special black people are a feature also of this stage.

The stage of autonomy enables an acceptance of racial differences and similarities to be dealt with appreciation and respect. This is accompanied by a perception that does not equate differences with deficiencies and an active seeking of opportunities for crossracial interactions.

The second model to be described is based upon the work of Atkinson et al. (1989) and has been termed the minority identity development model. Again, a five-stage model has been adopted, in the order: conformity, dissonance, resistance and immersion, introspection, and synergetic articulation and awareness.

The first stage of conformity is typified by members of minority groups identifying more strongly with dominant culture values, accompanied by a lack of awareness of an ethnic perspective. Negative attitudes are exhibited towards self and others of ethnic group origin and there is an acceptance of and belief in dominant group stereotypes about self and others.

During the dissonance stage, people experience confusion and conflict about their previously held values and they become aware of issues involving racism, sexism, oppression, etc. Feeling anger and loss they search for own-group role models with whom to identify.

The third stage of resistance and immersion involves active rejection and distrust of the dominant culture and greater identification with own culture. The immersion into their own culture involves interest in own-group history, traditions, foods, language, etc. A motivation to exhibit activist behaviour that is geared to challenging oppression emerges as well as a possible wish to separate from the dominant culture.

The fourth stage of introspection involves a questioning of their rigid rejection of the dominant group's values resulting in experiences of conflict and confusion regarding loyalty to one's own cultural group and personal autonomy. This is a struggle for self-awareness.

Synergetic articulation and awareness represent a stage of resolution of the above conflicts and offer a sense of fulfilment regarding personal cultural identity. Appreciation of other cultural groups as well as dominant group values is experienced, combined with a motivation to eliminate all forms of oppression.

Other models developed in this area include the Phinney model of adolescent ethnic identity development, Cross's model of black identity development, Kim's model of Asian-American identity development and Arce's model of chicano development. (These are all referenced and discussed in Ponterotto and Pedersen 1993.) All of this development and research work has been completed within the cultural context of the United States; no equivalent work has been carried out to our knowledge in the British context, a challenge indeed to British researchers.

Speight et al. (1991) cite several references that criticize these ethnic and racial identity development models as oversimplifying and relying on the notion of ethnic-cultural-racial pride. There are few models, they add, that address the complexity of individuals occupying positions of multiple oppression in society (e.g. persons of mixed-race heritage or of minority group heritage combined with, for example, non-dominant sexual preferences, etc.). This complexity of occupancy of multiple social positions within society requires 'researchers and therapists to interrogate their own position as much as those of their respondents and clients' (Phoenix 1994: 305).

Jewel's (1994) evaluation of multicultural counselling research includes a substantial section on research into racial identity development. He quotes Sue (1988), who points out that ethnicity *per se* tells us little about the attitudes, values, experiences and behaviour of individuals, therapists or clients who interact in a therapy session. Any research into ethnicity-matching between client and therapist is likely to produce weak or conflicting results. However, the meaning of ethnicity as it applies to both the client's and therapist's perceptions and expectations of each other and their cultural and linguistic capability may have more potential.

Helms and Carter (cited in Jewel 1994) have carried out a wide variety of research, based on the white racial identity model, that has included linking racial identity attitudes to counsellor preferences and including demographic (social class) effects. They have also attempted to establish theoretical models of how white clients respond to black counsellors.

Despite a wide range of research efforts, Jewel (1994: 20) quotes Abramowitz and Murray's tenet that 'no-one knows how prevalent race effects are in psychotherapy as it is practised today'. The results have been tentative because of the very complexity of the subject.

The two identity development models described above were introduced to the participants on a British training workshop in the summer of 1994, where they were enthusiastically received as a useful set of conceptualizations for counsellor consideration. Lee (1994), at the same conference, referred to the possibility of assessing the differential levels of counsellor and client attainment on the development models as a way of further understanding the possible dynamics that might emerge during therapy. Useful research, therefore, is not only required on generating cultural identity models for the British context but also on their value within the transcultural therapy process.

Research, clinical effectiveness and training

Lee and Richardson (1991), from the substantially more advanced American position on research, specify four major domains for research development. Underpinning these, they remind us that research evidence must guide multicultural counselling practice. Their four goals comprise the following:

1 The continuously evolving notions about multicultural counselling and human development should be empirically validated. Not only is new research needed on counselling process and outcomes but empirical evidence is also required to support ideas about the effectiveness of indigenous models of helping and the development of culturally responsive counselling interventions.
2 We need to construct culturally diverse notions of normal human development and to conduct investigations that assess mental health outcomes in relation to person–environment interactions among different groups.
3 Empirical investigations should be initiated to produce inventories that assess significant developmental aspects of specific cultural groups.
4 Research efforts should be structured to investigate intragroup differences among people. The majority of research evidence has been gathered without consideration of differences in factors such as level of ethnic identity, level of acculturation or socio-economic status.

The link between research and training is obviously an important relationship, where research can inform trainees and they in their turn may be stimulated towards new research. Research is also required on the efficacy of the training process itself in producing knowledgeable, aware and skilled counsellors. A research study by D'Andrea et al. (1991) cited by Jewel (1994: 25) suggested, for example, that 'it is more difficult to promote the acquisition of multicultural counselling skills than to improve students' cross-cultural awareness and knowledge.

A particular dichotomy exists between the general emphases of traditional counsellor training and transcultural counselling courses. The particular circumstances in Britain surrounding training have to be taken into account here as well (see Chapter 11). But, generally speaking, traditional counselling courses encourage inner awareness, study of therapeutic process, theoretical perspective and the enhancement of skills. Most courses do not concentrate on societal issues, personality types or specific clinical disorders that may be presented by clients. The focus is on the therapeutic process, whoever the client may be.

Short courses on transcultural therapy tend to encourage participants' understandings of various client groups, their relative position in society, the complex issues of personal and institutional power and the mechanisms of racism. Awareness training is geared towards comprehending the implications of projection, stereotyping, transference issues, etc. The focus here is on societal understanding with specific client groups, not on therapeutic process and skills. This tension between the two types of training is an interesting one.

Some training developments within transcultural counselling courses have included experimentation with role-play scenarios (similar to traditional counselling training) and use of video materials (Clark and Lago 1981). Pedersen's triad model, which was first developed in the 1970s, has had some impact upon training – though less so in Britain – and has subsequently been developed further (Pedersen 1988).

Research on the efficacy of specific training procedures and how these may contribute to ensuring an appropriate balance between knowledge, awareness and skills development in counselling students is urgently required.

Summing up

The whole research and training endeavour within transcultural counselling is suffused by a deep concern for ethical practice in relation to all clients living within a multiracial society. From an ethical perspective, 'counsellors and psychotherapists are obligated to protect clients from potential harm and prevent harm wherever possible (beneficence) and are equally responsible for not inflicting harm upon clients (non-maleficence)' (Lee and Kurilla 1993: 4).

This book addresses the substance of the very real challenges facing counsellors in a multiracial and multicultural society. We are concerned that counselling and psychotherapy does not become a further oppressive or damaging instrument of society but that it continues to aspire to be an appropriately liberating and therapeutic force for any troubled individuals, families or groups seeking psychological help and emotional support.

References

Albee, G.W. (1977) The Protestant ethic, sex and psychotherapy, *American Psychologist*, 32: 150–61.

Allen, S. (1973) The institutionalisation of racism, *RACE*, XV:(1).

American Field Services *Orientation Handbook Resource*. AFS Intercultural/International Programmes.

Argyle, M. (1975) *Bodily Communication*. London: Methuen.

Atkinson, D. (1985) A meta-review of research on cross-cultural counselling and psychotherapy, *Journal of Multicultural Counselling and Development*, 13: 138–53.

Atkinson, D., Morten, G. and Sue, D.W. (1989) *Counselling American Minorities: A Cross Cultural Perspective*. Dubuque, IA: William C. Brown.

Bachner, D.J. and Rudy, S.K. (1989) Organisational factors in cross-cultural counselling, in D.R. Koslow and E.P. Salett (eds) *Crossing Cultures in Mental Health*. Washington, DC: SIETAR.

Baker, K.G. (1989) A workshop model for exploring one's cultural identity, in D.R. Koslow and E.P. Salett (eds) *Crossing Cultures in Mental Health*. Washington, DC: SIETAR.

Bandura, A. (1969) *Principles of Behaviour Modification*. New York: Wiley.

Beattie, J. (1964) *Other Cultures: Aims, Methods and Achievements in Social Anthropology*. London: Routledge and Kegan Paul.

Becker, E. (1972) *The Birth and Death of Meaning*. Harmondsworth: Penguin.

Becker, H.S. and Gear, B. (1960) Latent culture: a note on the theory of latent social roles, *Administrative Science Quarterly*, 5: 304–13.

Benedict, R. (1968) *Patterns of Culture*. London: Routledge and Kegan Paul.

Ben Tovim, G. and Gabriel, J. (1982) The politics of race in Britain, 1962–79: a review of the major trends and of recent debates, in C. Husband (ed.) *Race in Britain: Continuity and Change*. London: Hutchinson.

Berne, E. (1968) *Games People Play*. Harmondsworth: Penguin.

Bernstein, B. (1973) *Class Codes and Control*. London: Routledge and Kegan Paul.

Bourdieu, P. (1976) Systems of education and systems of thought, in R. Dale, G. Esland and M. Macdonald (eds) *Schooling and Capitalism*. London: Routledge and Kegan Paul.

Boyd-Franklin, N. (1989) *Black Families in Therapy: A Multisystems Approach*. New York: Guilford Press.

Bram, R.W. (1956) Language and categories in J.S. Bruner, J.J. Goodnow and G.A. Austin (eds) *A Study in Thinking*. New York: Wiley.

Brislin, R.W., Cushner, K., Cherrie, C. and Yong, M. (1986) *Intercultural Interactions: A Practical Guide*. Beverly Hills, CA: Sage.

British Association for Counselling (1987) *Code of Ethics and Practice for the Supervision of Counsellors*. Rugby: British Association for Counselling.

British Association for Counselling (1992) *Invitation to Membership*. Rugby: British Association for Counselling.

Brown, C. (1984) *Black and White Britain: The Third PSI Survey*. Aldershot: Gower.

Byham, W.C. and Cox, J. (1988) *Zapp, the Lightning of Empowerment*. New York: Fawcett Columbine.

Carotenuto, A. (1992) *The Difficult Art: A Critical Discourse on Psychotherapy*. Wilmetter, IL: Chiron.

Carroll, M. (1988) Counselling supervision: the British Context, *Counselling Psychology Quarterly*, 1(4): 387–96.

Casse, P. (1981) *Training for the Cross Cultural Mind*. Washington, DC: SIETAR.

Chen, C. (1963) Some psychopathological thoughts in the book of Tso Chuen, *Acta Psychologica Sinica*, 2: 156–64.

Chertok, L. (1984) 200 years of psychotherapy: the curative elements in suggestion and affect, *Psychoanalytic Psychology*, 1(3): 173–91.

Clark, J. (1982) Change is boundaries dissolved: person-centred approaches in a multi-racial society, in S.A. Segrera (ed.) *Proceedings of the 1st International Forum on the Person-Centred Approach*, pp. 303–14. Mexico: Universidad Iberoamericana.

Clark, J. and Lago, C.O. (1981) 'Multi-racial videoscenes', video and training manual. Leicester: Department of Educational Technology, Leicester Polytechnic.

Clark, R.W. (1980) *Freud: The Man and the Cause*. London: Cape and Weidenfeld and Nicolson.

Collinson, L. (1984) Transactional analysis, in W. Dryden (ed.) *Individual Therapy in Britain*. London: Harper and Row.

Cook, D. (1983) 'A survey of ethnic minority clinical and counselling graduate student perceptions of their cross-cultural supervision experience', Unpublished Doctoral Dissertation. Southern Illinois University.

Cooper, C. (1984) Individual therapies: limitations, in W. Dryden (ed.) *Individual Therapy in Britain*. London: Harper and Row.

Cox, C.I. (1982) 'Outcome research in cross-cultural counselling, unpublished manuscript.

Cox, C. (1988) 'Acculturative stress and world view', unpublished doctoral dissertation. Ohio State University.

Crandel, D.L. and Dohrenwend, B.P. (1967) Some relations among psychiatric symptoms, organic illness and social class. *American Journal of Psychiatry*, 123: 527–38.

D'Andrea, M., Daniels, J. and Beck, R. (1991) Evaluating the impact of multicultural counsellor training, *Journal of Counselling and Development*, 70: 143–50.

D'Ardenne, P. and Mahtani, A. (1989) *Transcultural Counselling in Action*. London: Sage.

De Marré, P.B. (1975) The politics of large groups, in L. Kreeger (ed.) *The Large Group: Dynamics ad Therapy*. London: Constable.

Dryden, W. (ed.) (1984) *Individual Therapy in Britain*. London: Harper and Row.

Dryden, W. (1990) Counselling under apartheid: an interview with Andrew Swart, *British Journal of Guidance and Counselling*, 18(3), September.

Dryden, W. and Spurling, L. (1989) *On Becoming a Psychotherapist*. London: Tavistock/Routledge.

Dryden, W. and Thorne, B. (eds) (1991) *Training and Supervision for Counselling in Action*. London: Sage.

Eibl-Eibesfeldt, I. (1972) Similarities and differences between cultures in expressive movements, in R.A. Hinde (ed.) *Non-Verbal Communication*. Cambridge: Royal Society and Cambridge University Press.

Eleftheriadou, Z. (1994) *Transcultural Counselling*. London: Central Books.

Ellenberger, H.F. (1970) *The Discovery of the Unconscious: The History and Evolution of Dynamic Psychiatry*. London: Allen Lane.

Ellsworth, E. (1989) Why doesn't this feel empowering? Working through the repressive myths of critical pedagogy. *Harvard Educational Review*, 50: 297–324.

Feltham, C. and Dryden, W. (1993) *Dictionary of Counselling*. London: Whurr.

Fernando, S. (1988) *Race and Culture in Psychiatry*. London: Croom Helm.

Flew, A. (1972) *An Introduction to Western Philosophy: Ideas and Argument from Plato to Sartre*. London: Thames and Hudson.

Frank, J.D. (1973) *Persuasion and Healing: A Comparative Study of Psychotherapy*. Baltimore, MD: Johns Hopkins University Press.

Fransella, F. (1984) Personal Construct Therapy in W. Dryden (ed.) *Individual Therapy In Britain*. London: Harper and Row.

Freire, P. (1972) *Pedagogy of the Oppressed*. Harmondsworth: Penguin.

Frijda, N. and Johoda, G. (1969) On the scope and methods of cross-cultural research, in D.R. Price-Williams (ed.) *Cross-Cultural Studies*. Harmondsworth: Penguin.

Fryer, P. (1984) *Staying Power: The History of Black People in Britain*. London: Pluto.

Furnham, A. and Bochner, S. (1986) *Culture Shock: Psychological Reactions to Unfamiliar Environments*. London: Methuen.

Garfield, S. and Kurtz, R. (1976) Clinical Psychologists in the 1970's, *American Psychologist*, 31: 1–9.

Gopaul-McNicol, S.A. (1993) *Working with West Indian Families*. New York: Guilford Press.

Gore, J. (1993) *The Struggle for Pedagogies*. London: Routledge.

Guardian (1994) Labour figures show rise in reported race attacks in London. 18 March.

Gudykunst, W.B. (1994) *Bridging Differences: Effective Intergroup Communication*, 2nd edn. London: Sage.

Guitterez, F. (1982) Working with minority counsellor education students, *Counsellor Education and Supervision*, 21: 218–26.

Gumperz, J.J., Jupp, T.C. and Roberts, C. (1981) 'Cross-Talk' – The Wider Perspective. Southall: Industrial Language Training Laboratory.

Gurnah, A. (1992) On the specificity of racism, in M. Arnot and L. Barton (eds) *Voicing Concerns*. Oxford: Triangle Books.

Hall, E.T. (1959) *The Silent Language*. New York: Anchor Press/Doubleday.

Hall, E.T. (1966) *The Hidden Dimension*. New York: Anchor Press/Doubleday.

Hall, E.T. (1976a) *Beyond Culture*. New York: Anchor Press/Doubleday.

Hall, E.T. (1976b) How culture's collide, *Psychology Today*, July: 66–74.

Hall, E.T. (1983) *The Dance of Life*. New York: Anchor Press/Doubleday.

Hammon, D. and Jablow, A. (1970) *The Africa That Never Was: Four Centuries of British Writing about Africa*. New York: Twange.

Harner, M. (1990) *The Way of the Shaman*. San Francisco: Harper and Row.

Hartmann, P. and Husband, C. (1974) *Racism and the Mass-Media*. London: Davis-Pointer.

Hawkins, P. and Shohet, R. (1989) *Supervision in the Helping Professions*. Milton Keynes: Open University Press.

Helms, J. (1982) 'Differential evaluations of minority and majority counselling trainees practicum performance', unpublished manuscript. University of Maryland.

Helms, J.E. (1984) Towards a theoretical model of the effects of race on counselling: a black and white model. *The Counselling Psychologist*, 12: 153–65.

Herr, E.L. (1987) Cultural diversity from an international perspective. *Journal of Multicultural Counselling and Development*, 15: 99–109.

Hess, A. (1982) *Psychotherapy Supervision: Theory, Research and Practice*. New York: Witney.

Hesse, H. (1979) *The Glass Bead Game*. Harmondsworth: Penguin.

Hillmann, J. and Ventura, M. (1992) *We've Had 100 Years of Psychotherapy and the World is Getting Worse*. San Francisco: Harper.

Hiro, D. (1971) *Black British, White British*. Harmondsworth: Penguin.

Hobbs, G. (1993) White magic: in South Africa a growing number of white people are being initiated as witch doctors. *Observer Magazine*, 29 August.

Hofstede, G. (1980) *Cultures Consequences: International Differences in Work Related Values*. Beverly Hills, CA: Sage.

Holloway, E. and Hosford, R. (1983) Towards developing a prescriptive technology of counsellor supervision, *The Counselling Psychologist*, 11(1): 73–7.

Home Affairs Committee (1986) *Racial Attacks and Harassment*. London: HMSO.

Hunt. P. (1987) Black client: implications for supervision of trainees, *Psychotherapy*, 24(1): 114–19.

Ibrahim, F.A. (1985) Effective cross-cultural counselling and psychotherapy: a framework. *The Counselling Psychologist*, 13: 625–38.

Ivey, A.E. (1982) *International Interviewing and Counselling*. Monterey, CA: Brooks/Cole.

Jackson, A.P. and Meadows, F.B. (1991) Getting to the bottom to understand the top. *Journal of Counselling and Development*. Sept/Oct: 72–6.

Jacobs, M. (1984) Psychodynamic therapy: the Freudian approach, in W. Dryden (ed.) *Individual Therapy in Britain*. London: Harper and Row.

Jacobs, M. (1992) *Sigmund Freud*. London: Sage.

Jewel, P. (1994) Multicultural counselling research: an evaluation with proposals for future research, *Counselling Psychology Review*, 9(2), May.

Jilek, W.G. (1989) Therapeutic use of altered states of consciousness in contemporary North American dance ceremonials, in C.A. Ward (ed.) *Altered States of Consciousness and Mental Health: A Cross-Cultural Perspective*. London: Sage.

Jones, E. (ed.) (1959) *Sigmund Freud: Collected Papers*, Vol. 1. New York: Basic Books.

Jones, E.E. (1987) Psychotherapy and counselling with black clients, in P. Pedersen (ed). *Handbook of Cross-Cultural Counselling and Therapy*. New York: Praeger.

Jordan, W.D. (1982) First impressions: initial English confrontations with Africans, in C. Husband (ed.) *Race in Britain: Continuity and Change*. London: Hutchinson.

Jowell, R., Witherspoon, S. and Brook, L. (1984) *British Social Attitudes: The 1984 Report*. Aldershot: Gower/Social and Community Planning Research.

Jumaa, M. (1993) From the chair, *RACE Newsletter*, December, 3. Rugby: British Association for Counselling.

Kanfer, F.H. and Phillips, J.W. (1970) *Learning Foundations of Behavior Therapy*. New York: Wiley.

Karasu, T. et al. (1984) *The Psychological Therapies*. Washington, DC: American Psychiatric Press.

Kardiner, A. (1947) *The Individual and This Society*. New York: Columbia University Press.

Kardiner, A. (1959) *The Psychological Frontiers of Society*. New York: Columbia University Press.

Kareem, J. (1978) Conflicting concepts of mental health in multi-cultural society. *Psyhiatrica Clinica*, 11: 90–5.

Kareem, J. and Littlewood, R. (1992) *Intercultural Therapy: Themes, Interpretations and Practices*. Oxford: Blackwell Scientific.

Katz, J.H. (1978) *White Awareness: A Handbook for Anti-Racism Training*. Norman, OK: University of Oklahoma Press.

Katz, J.H. (1985) The sociopolitical nature of counselling, *The Counselling Psychologist*, 13: 615–24.

Katz, R. (1989) Healing and transformation: perspectives from !Kung hunter–gatherers, in C.A. Ward (ed.) *Altered States of Consciousness and Mental Health: A Cross Cultural Perspective*. Newbury Park, CA: Sage.

Kemal, A. (1994) Sufism: a prevention and cure, *Changes: An International Journal of Psychology and Psychotherapy*, 12(2), June: 87–91.

Kirschenbaum, H. (1979) *On Becoming Carl Rogers*. New York: Delacort.

Kluckholm, C. and Murray, H.A. (1953) Personality formation: the determinants, in C. Kluckholm, H.A. Murray and D.M. Schneider (eds) *Personality in Nature, Society and Culture*. New York: Random House.

Kolko, D.J. (1987) Simplified inpatient treatment of nocturnal enureses in psychiatrically disturbed children, *Behaviour Therapy*, 2: 99–112.

Koslow, D.R. and Salett, E.P. (eds) (1989) *Crossing Cultures in Mental Health*. Washington, DC: SIETAR.

Kuhn, T. (1962) *The Structure of Scientific Revolutions*. Chicago: University of Chicago Press.

La Barre, W. (1964) Paralinguistics, kinesics and cultural anthropology, in T.A. Sebeok (ed.) *Approaches to Semiotics*. The Hague: Moulton.

Lago, C.O. (1990) *Working with Overseas Students: A Staff Development Training Manual*. Huddersfield: Huddersfield University and British Council.

Lago, C.O. (1992) Some complexities in counselling international students. *Journal of International Education*, 3(1) March: 21–34.

Lago, C.O. (1994) Therapy for a masturbatory society: the need for connectedness. *Counselling*, 5(2), May: 120–4.

Lago, C.O. and Thompson, J. (1989a) Counselling and race, in W. Dryden, D. Charles-Edwards and R. Wolfe (eds) *Handbook of Counselling in Britain*. London: Tavistock-Routledge.

Lago, C.O. and Thompson, J. (1989b) 'Issues of race and culture in counselling settings: video and training manual. University of Leicester: Audio Visual Services, (video). (1991) London: Barr Publications (manual).

Lago, H.M. (1994) 'The implications of empowerment with respect to accountability, training, costs, benefits and problems and the effect on management's role, pp. 120–4, unpublished MBA essay. University of Surrey.

Larson, P.C. (1982) Counselling special populations, *Professional Psychology*, 12(6): 843–58.

Lee, C. (1994) Introductory lecture to a conference on race, culture and counselling. (Unpublished) University of Sheffield, July.

Lee, C.C. and Richardson, B.L. (1991) *Multicultural Issues in Counselling: New Approaches to Diversity*. Alexandria, VA: American Association for Counselling and Development.

Lee, C.C., Oh, M.Y. and Mountcastle, A.R. (1992) Indigenous models of helping in non-western countries: implications for multicultural counselling, *Journal of Multicultural Counselling and Development*, 20 January: 3–10.

Lee, C.C. and Kurilla, V. (1993) Ethics and multi-culturalism: the challenge of diversity, *Ethical Issues in Professional Counselling*, 1(3): 1–11.

Leff, J.P. (1973) Culture and the differentiation of emotional states. *British Journal of Psychiatry*, 123: 299–306.

Lehmann, P. (1994) Progressive psychiatry: publisher J.F. Lehmann as promoter of social psychiatry under fascism. *Changes: The Journal of the Psychology and Psychotherapy Association*, 12(1): 37–49.

Le Page, R.B. (1968) Problems of description in multi-lingual communities. *Transactions of the Philological Society Journal*, 189–212.

Linton, R. (1945) *The Cultural Background of Personality*. New York: Harper and Row.

Loganbill, C., Hardy, C. and Delworth, U. (1982) Supervision: a conceptual model, *The Counselling Psychologist*, 10(1): 3–42.

Lyons, C.H. (1975) *To Wash an Aethiop White: British Ideas about Black African Educability, 1530–1860*. New York: Teachers College Press.

McCarthy, P., Debell, C., Kanuha, V. and McLeod, J. (1988) Myths of supervision, identifying the gaps between theory and practice. *Counsellor Education and Supervision*, 28: 22–8.

Mackay, D. (1984) Behavioural psychotherapy, in W. Dryden (ed.) *Individual Therapy in Britain*. London: Harper and Row.

Mactaggart, F. and Gostin, L. (1983) Letter to the *Guardian* (reporting findings by the Joint Council for the Welfare of Immigrants and the National Council for Civil Liberties).

Mahrer, A. (1989) *The Integration of Psychotherapies: A Guide for Practising Therapists*. New York: Human Science Press.

Mandelbaum, D.G. (ed.) (1940) *Selected Writings of Edward Sapir*. London: Cambridge University Press.

Maw, J. (1980) Lecture on the experience of African students in the United Kingdom. University of London, June.

McDevitt, C. (1994) 'Countertransference issues in working with students from other European cultures, paper presented to the FEDORA (European Association of Guidance and Counselling) conference, Barcelona.

McGrath, P. and Axelson, J.A. (1993) *Accessing Awareness and Developing Knowledge: Foundations for Skills in a Multicultural Society*. Monterey, CA: Brooks/Cole.

McLeod, J. (1993) *An Introduction to Counselling*. Buckingham: Open University.

Mearns, D. (1994) *Developing Person-Centred Counselling*. London: Sage.

Moodley, R. (1991) 'Interpreting the "I" in counselling and guidance: an anti-racist approach', unpublished text of lecture.

Morgan, W.J. and Bo, J. (1993) Why should overseas students return to their home countries? *Journal of International Education*, July, 4(2): 66–70.

Murphy, H.B.M. (1986) The mental health impact of British cultural traditions, in J.L. Cox (ed.) *Transcultural Psychiatry*. London: Croom Helm.

Myers, L. (1988) *Understanding an Afrocentric World View: Introduction to an Optimal Psychology*. Dubuque, IA: Kendall/Hunt.

Neely, K. (1995) Suicide on the net, *Guardian*, 6 January.

Nelson-Jones, R. (1988) *The Theory and Practice of Counselling Psychology*. London: Cassell.

Neville, B. (1994) 'Five kinds of empathy', paper presented to the Third International Conference on Client-Centred and Experiential Psychotherapy. Gmunden, Austria.

Orbach, S. (1993) Behind the political psyche, *Weekend Guardian*, November.

Owen, D. (1993) *Analysis of the 1991 Census*. University of Warwick, Centre for Research in Ethnic Relations.

Palmer, M. (1991) *The Elements of Taoism*. London: Element.

Paniagua, F.A. (1994) *Assessing and Treating Culturally Diverse Clients: A Practical Guide*. London: Sage.

Park, L.C. and Covi, L. (1965) Nonblind placebo trial, *Archives of General Psychiatry*, 12 April: 336–45.

Pedersen, P.B. (1987) Ten frequent assumptions of cultural bias in counselling, *Journal of Multicultural Counselling and Development*, January: 16–24.

Pedersen, P.B. (1988) *Handbook for Developing Multicultural Awareness*. Alexandria, VA: American Counselling Association.

Pedersen, P.B. (1991) Multiculturalism as a generic approach to counselling, *Journal of Counselling and Development*, Sept/Oct, 70: 6–12.

Pedersen, P.B. (1994) *A Handbook for Developing Multicultural Awareness*. Alexandria, VA: American Counselling Association.

Pedersen, P.B., Draguns, J.G., Lonner, W.J. and Trimble, J.E. (1981) *Counselling Across Cultures*. Hawaii: East-West Center.

Phoenix, A. (1994) Research: positioned differently? Issues of race, difference and commonality, *Changes*, 12(4): 299–305.

Phung, T.C. (1995) An experience of inter-cultural counselling: views from a black client, *Counselling: The Journal of the British Association for Counselling*, February, 6(1): 61–2.

Pilgrim, D. (1992) Psychotherapy and political evasions, in W. Dryden, and C. Feltham (eds) *Psychotherapy and its Discontents*. Buckingham: Open University Press.

Pinker, S. (1994) *The Language Instinct: The New Science of Language and Mind*. London: Allen Lane.

Ponterotto, J.G. and Pedersen, P.B. (1993) *Preventing Prejudice: A Guide for Counsellors and Educators*. Newbury Park, CA: Sage.

Power, G. (1981) 'The language of ethnic minority groups with special reference to education', paper given at a conference on Education and Cultural Diversity. Homerton College, Cambridge, June.

Proctor, B. (1989) *Supervision: A Working Alliance*. London: Alexia.

Raboteau, A.J. (1986) The Afro-American traditions, in R.L. Numbers and D.W. Amundsen (eds) *Caring and Curing: Health and Medicine in the Western Religious Traditions*. New York: Macmillan.

Rees, T. (1982) Immigration policies in the United Kingdom, in C. Husband (ed.) *Race in Britain: Continuity and Change*. London: Hutchinson.

Relate (1992) *History of the National Marriage Guidance Council,* Now Known as Relate, Information paper. Rugby: Relate.

Ridley, C.R. (1995) *Overcoming Unintentional Racism in Counselling and Therapy.* London: Sage.

Rogers, C.R. (1959) A theory of therapy, personality and interpersonal relationships as developed in the client-centred framework, in S. Koch (ed.) *Psychology: A Study of Science.* New York: McGraw-Hill.

Rogers, C.R. (1969) *Freedom to Learn: A View of What Education Might Become.* Columbus, OH: Charles E. Merrill Publishing Co.

Rogers, C.R. (1980) *A Way of Being.* Boston, MA: Houghton Mifflin.

Rogers, C.R. (1987) *Client-Centred Therapy.* London: Constable.

Romaine, S. (1994) *Language in Society: An Introduction to Sociolinguistics.* Oxford: Oxford University Press.

Samuels, A. (1985) *Jung and the Post-Jungians.* London: Tavistock/Routledge.

Samuels, A. (1993) *The Political Psyche.* London: Routledge.

Sanders, C. (1994) Most immigrants are white, *Times Higher Education Supplement.* 21 January, p. 5.

Sapir, E. (1931) Conceptual categories of primitive languages. *Science,* 74.

Sarup, M. (1978) *Marxism and Education.* London: Routledge and Kegan Paul.

Scheutz, A. (1944) The stranger: an essay in social psychology, *American Journal of Sociology,* 49: 499–507.

Scull, A. (1975) From madness to mental illness: medical men as moral entrepreneurs, *European Journal of Sociology,* 16: 218–61.

Scull, A. (1979) *Museums of Madness: The Social Organisation of Insanity in Nineteenth Century England.* London: Allen Lane.

Sharrock, W.W. and Anderson, D.C. (1981) Language, thought and reality, again, *Journal of British Sociological Association,* 15(2): 287–93.

Skellington, R. and Morris, P. (1992) *Race in Britain Today.* London: Sage and Open University.

Smith, D.J. (1977) *Racial Disadvantage in Britain: The PEP Report.* Harmondsworth: Penguin.

Speight, S.L., Myers, L.J., Cox, C.I. and Highlen, P.S. (1991) A redefinition, *Journal of Counselling and Development,* 70, Sept./Oct.: 29–36.

Staub, E. (1993) The psychology of bystanders, perpetrators and heroic helpers. *International Journal of Intercultural Relations,* 17(3): 315–41.

Stringer, S. (1992) Home is where the heart is, *Counselling News,* 8 December.

Sue, D.W. (1981) *Counselling the Culturally Different: Theory and Practice.* New York: Wiley.

Sue, D.W., Arrendondo, P., and McDavis, R.J. (1992) Multicultural counselling competencies and standards: a call to the profession, *Journal of Counselling and Development,* March/April, 70: 477–86.

Sue, D.W., Bernie, J.E., Durran, A., Freinberg, L., Pedersen, P., Smith, E.H. and Vasquez-Nuttall, E. (1982) Position paper: cross cultural competencies, *The Counselling Psychologist,* 10: 1–8.

Sue, S. (1988) Psychotherapist service for ethnic minorities, *American Psychologist,* 43(4): 301–8.

Sutton, C. (1987) *Handbook of Research for the Helping Professions.* London: Routledge and Kegan Paul.

Szasz, T. (1970) *The Manufacture of Madness: A Comparative Study of the Inquisition and the Mental Health Movement.* New York: Harper and Row.

Szasz, T. (1971) The sane slave, *American Journal of Psychotherapy*, 25, April: 228–39.

Thomas, A. and Sillen, S. (1972) *Racism and Psychiatry*. New York: Bruner and Mazell.

Thompson, H. (1992) The context of abuse and deprivation, *Counselling: The Journal of the British Association for Counselling*, November, 3(4): 225–8.

Thompson, J. (1991) 'Issues of race and culture in counselling supervision training courses', unpublished MSc thesis. Polytechnic of East London.

Thorne, B. (1984) Person-centred therapy, in W. Dryden (ed.) *Individual Therapy in Britain*. London: Harper and Row.

Torrey, E.F. (1972) *The Mind Game: Witch Doctors and Psychiatrists*. New York: Emerson-Hall.

Triandis (1975) Culture training, cognitive complexity and interpersonal attitudes, in R.W. Brislin, S. Bocher, and W.J. Lonner (eds) *Cross Cultural Perspectives on Learning*. New York: Wiley.

Troyna, B. (1981) *Public Awareness and the Media: A Study of Reporting on Race*. London: Commission for Racial Equality.

Troyna, B. (1993) *Racism and Education: Research Perspectives*. Buckingham: Open University.

Troyna, B. (1994) 'Blind faith? Empowerment and educational research, paper presented to the International Sociology of Education Conference. Sheffield University, 4–6 January.

Tseng, W.S. (1986) Chinese Psychiatry: development and characteristics in J.L. Cox (ed.) *Transcultural Psychiatry*. London: Croom Helm.

Tseng, W. and Hsu, J. (1979) Culture and psychotherapy, in A.J. Marsella, R. Thorp and T. Ciborowski (eds) *Perspectives on Cross-Cultural Psychology*. New York: Academic Press.

Turner, V. (1967) *The Forest of Symbols: Aspects of Ndembu Ritual*. Ithaca, NY: Cornell University Press.

Tyler, E.B. (1903) *Primitive Cultures*, 4th revised edn. London: Murray.

Valentine, C.A. (1968) *Culture and Poverty*. Chicago: University of Chicago Press.

Valla, J.P. and Prince, R.H. (1989) Religious experiences as self-healing mechanisms, in C.A. Ward (ed.) *Altered States of Consciousness and Mental Health: A Cross-Cultural Perspective*. London: Sage.

Vandervolk, C. (1974) The relationship of personality, values and race to anticipation of the supervisory relationship. *Rehabilitation Counselling Bulletin*, 18: 41–6.

Van Dijk, T.A. (1993) *Elite Discourse and Racism*. London: Sage.

van Deurzen-Smith, E. (1984) Existential therapy, in W. Dryden (ed.) *Individual Therapy in Britain*. London: Harper and Row.

Vaughan, M. (1977) Overseas students: some cultural clues, *UKCOSA News*, 9(1), Spring/Summer.

Walker, R.D. and La Due, R. (1986) An integrative approach to American Indian mental health, in C.R. Wilkinson (ed.) *Ethnic Psychiatry*. New York: Plenum.

Ward, C.A. (ed.) (1989) *Altered States of Consciousness and Mental Health: A Cross-Cultural Perspective*. London: Sage.

Watson, J. and Rayner, R. (1920) Conditional emotional reactions, *Journal of Experimental Psychology*, 3: 1–14.

Webb Johnson, A. (1993) Cultural divide, *Counselling News*, 9 March: 26–7.

Westwood, M.J. (1990) 'Identification of human problems and methods of help seeking: a cross cultural study', paper presented to the Comparative and International Education Society. Anaheim, California, 29 March to 1 April.

Whorf, B.L. (1956) Language, mind and reality, in J.B. Carroll and Carroll (eds) *Language, Thought and Reality*. Cambridge, MA: MIT Press.

Williams, R. (1983) *Keywords: A Vocabulary of Culture and Society*. London: Fontana.

Wittkower, E.D. (1970) Trance and possession states, *International Journal of Social Psychiatry*, 16: 153–60.

Wolpe, J. (1958) *Psychotherapy by Reciprocal Inhibition*. Stamford, NY: Stamford University Press.

Wood, J.K. (1990) 'Everything and nothing: client-centred therapy, the person-centred approach and beyond' privately published document.

Yeaxlee, B.A. (1925) *Spiritual Values in Adult Education*. London: Oxford University Press.

Yui, L. (1978) 'Degree of assimilation and its effect on the preference of counselling style and of self-disclosure among Chinese Americans in Hawaii', unpublished doctoral dissertation. Indiana University.

Index

COUNSELLING FOR WOMEN

Janet Perry

Although few in number, organizations which provide counselling services for women have had a tremendous impact on our current understanding of women's psychology and the issues women explore in counselling. Through her examination of these organizations, Janet Perry highlights the unique emphasis they place on the importance of how services are provided and their exploration of the dynamics of the working relationships of women counsellors. The organizations included in the book range from Women's Aid to Women's Therapy Centres and their services are considered in the context of counselling women. The study shows that through a self-reflexive examination of their organizational processes, these agencies have come to a greater understanding of the ways in which women working with women create non-hierarchical and cooperative endeavours, much needed in our individualistic and competitive society. The book illustrates the conflicts that arise when both modes seek to exist within one organization – Family Service Units – and the struggle all the agencies have to legitimize these ways of working to a male dominated system from which funding is often sought. Recommended reading for all those involved in counselling and psychotherapy, this book illustrates some of the practical outcomes of these alternative working models.

Contents
The development of counselling in women's organizations – Counselling in women's organizations – The practice of counselling women – Specific issues in counselling women – Professional relationships in counselling for women – A critique of counselling for women – References – Index.

128 pp   0 335 19034 0 (paperback)

COUNSELLING FOR YOUNG PEOPLE

Judith Mabey and Bernice Sorensen

This book gives a wide picture of the diversity of counselling services available to young people in Britain today, with special focus on schools and young people's counselling services. It sets these services in their historical context and describes how they have evolved. The book puts forward theoretical models for working with young clients and discusses counselling issues as they relate to work with this age group. In addition it considers some of the pitfalls counsellors may encounter in working alongside other professionals and within agencies. It includes discussion on ethical issues, non-discriminatory practice, confidentiality and child protection. The book is enlivened by case material and by examples of good practice and interesting initiatives from around the country. It will be of particular interest to counsellors, teachers, youth workers, social workers and counselling students interested in working with this age group.

Features
- Illustrated throughout with case material
- Wide discussion of ethical issues
- Examples of good practice and new initiatives
- Gives theoretical models for counselling young people

Contents
The development of counselling for young people – Counselling for young people – The practice of counselling for young people – Specific issues in counselling for young people – Professional relationships in counselling for young people – A critique of counselling for young people – Appendix – References – Index.

160 pp   0 335 19298 X (paperback)